MAGICK

Judie Hall and her protective magickal dagger at 'The Gathering' as Jonny Depp's mystical Tonto

SPELLING IT OUT - THE EDITORS RAVE
THE ONE TRUE WAY

Why Do Modern Occult Groups Want To Think That They Are the One Who Invented the Wheel?

Millennials think they invented the cliterous & modern occultists think they invented magick. Sorry to tell you this guys, they both may be illusive but they have always been there! Both are just a part of being human.

It used to only be the big 5 that claimed exclusive revelation but now we are seeing the rise of competing occult groups that promulgate similar ideas. Magick deals with universal principals, for instance, you don't have to be a scientist to know that gravity works. Books, teachers & groups may help you get there, conversely you may have gotten there before them. People can work magick without rising through the ranks of an organisation. Similarly, all spirituality is a private path that follows the road of personal understanding. You set the pace. The amount that you connect with your higher-self will determine how far you are lead down the magickal path whether you work with a group or solitary. You will not get something until experiences in your life make that relevant for you. Sometimes it can be explained to you. A teacher can help you have that 'Aha!' moment. Yet teachers and prophets can show the way only because they have the elevated view from the vantage point of standing on another giant's shoulders. All prophets had a prophet. Buddha came out of Hinduism, Jesus blended Judaism with Buddhism, Mohamed blended Bedouin culture with Christian ideals. 20thC occultists had Dr. L. W. deLaurence. Lauron William deLaurence published over 80 occult works, a decade before the famous names began writing on the occult. He co-authored with his fellow Chicago resident, the respected William Walker Atkinson. These books have become the basis of most modern western occultist traditions. His concepts were so integrated in to western Vuodo, Hoodoo & Obeah, that these traditions would not exist in their present form if it wasn't for his work.

He was so successful that according to the most recent regulations of the Jamaica Customs "*All publications of de Laurence Scott & Company of Chicago in the United States of America relating to divination, magic, cultism or supernatural arts,*" are prohibited from entering the country to this day!

His officious faux-Old English writing style has been plagiarised by Waite & Crowley. He has been accused of pirating Waite's Tarot & Mathers/Crowley's Goetia, yet, the truth is that both Mathers & Waite were notoriously terrible with money & had shopped their manuscripts to many occult publishing houses. deLaurence was the largest esoteric publisher of his day. It still exists today 125 years later! So of cause they would have approached the deLaurence company & most likely struck a deal as there has never been a legal suit against him for a breach of copyright.

My point is this, no one has the right to say that there is only one true magickal way, even though deLaurence did (see extract form his writing pictured here) The admonition to be silent to avoid the 'wolves in sheep clothing,' which several later occult groups lifted from deLaurence almost word for word, serves to prevent discussion that might reveal what they don't know. If you can't discuss it with anyone then they have you. We grow when we share and discuss. I recently had the unfortunate experience of trying to discuss 'things they didn't understand,' with a long established magickal order, whose tenets of 'silence' keep them locked in the past. If any speaks out, it is a case of 'The Emperor's New Clothes:' 'only a fool or an innocent would dare say there's really nothing there.' Well, in my foolish innocence I have created this magazine to share info & spark discussion. We love hearing back from you & if you can teach me something new as well then we both win and are evolving the world magickally.

Magick Magazine No. 8

TABLE OF CONTENTS

Our theme this issue is PROTECTION MAGICK. Protection charms are our most requested spells. So sit back. RELAX. The Magick Magazine team has you covered!

SPELLING IT OUT - THE EDITORS RAVE - THE ONE TRUE WAY	2	PURIFICATION OF AUTUMN	42
TABLE OF CONTENTS	3	AUTUMN FIRE RITUAL TO HESTIA	43
CREATING BOUNDARIES TO PROTECT	5	MENTAL POISONING & BLACK MAGIC	44
A LONG LINE OF INTUITIVE WOMEN	7	THE WOMAN WHO DISCOVERED WHAT THE UNIVERSE IS MADE OF	48
ANNA'S SIMPLE PROTECTION SPELL	8	THE RED GODDESS	50
THE GATHERING 2018	9	THE WEEKLY SEER	51
A HEALING ARTIST	10	NOSTRADAMUS' PROPHECIES	52
PROTECTION SPELLS	12	TASSEOGRAPHY	54
A WITCHES HOME	14	MAGIC IS 'ALL' AROUND	55
FIONA HORNE SPEAKS	17	CALLING ALL MAGICKAL EMPATHS	56
DRAGONS BLOOD - THE SCENT OF PROTECTION	23	NEPTUNES SCEPTER PART 2 - EROTIC PAGAN FICTION	58
THE ART OF PYROGRAPHY	24	THE SOUTHERN & NORTHERN WITCH'S ALMANAC JAN - MAY 2019	61
THE WITCHES MARKET 2018	27	HELP PAGANISM TO BECOME A RECOGNISED DENOMINATION IN AUSTRALIA	65
HERMETIC INVOCATION TO HERMES - GOD OF MAGICK	28	THE WITCH'S BALL 2018	66
FAIRYTOPIA 2018	30	FUNNY PAGES - THE SUMMONED MAGICKAL MUSIC - ATH93	68
DAMIEN ECHOLS - MAGICK WILL SET YOU FREE	32	ART AS MAGICK	69
KONX OM PAX	38	OUR LAST CAPTION COMPETITION	70
CROSS WORD - PROTECTION MAGICK	40	MAGICKAL EVENTS	71
LORDE "IM BASICALLY A WITCH" THE ART OF BOWIE	41		

LEFT: Handsome, successful, wildly wealthy & innovative, L.W. deLaurence walked his talk and was more responsible than any other for making magick accessible to popular Western culture. BELOW: L.W. de Laurence's writing style & admonition to be silent. RIGHT: His business logo & colours have been copied by several occult traditions

More on L. W. de Laurence in our next issue

Therefore, my good friend, whosoever thou art, that desirest to accomplish these things, be but persuaded first to apply thyself to the ETERNAL WISDOM, entreating wisdom to grant thee understanding, then seeking knowledge with diligence, and thou shalt never repent thy having taken so laudable a resolution, but thou shalt enjoy a secret happiness and serenity of soul, which the world can never rob thee of.

Wishing thee every success imaginable in thy studies and experiments, hoping that thou wilt use the benefits that thou mayest receive to the honor of thy Creator and my Brother Adepts both in Spirit and Earth Life who have so ably assisted me in placing this knowledge before thee my friend and for the benefit of thy neighbor, in which exercise thou shalt ever experience the satisfaction of doing thy duty; remember my instructions—to be silent; talk only with those worthy of thy communication—do not give pearls to swine; be friendly to all, but not familiar with all; for many are—wolves in sheep clothing.

L. W. de Laurence.

Magick spelled with a "K," in the old Scottish fashion, indicates a number of belief systems that teach how to make changes in the external world according to your will. The "k" makes a distinction between deeply held beliefs & mere stage prestidigitation or trickery, as is indicated when spelled as "magic."

Proudly Australian owned, operated & produced. A not-for-profit publication. Contributed articles are not the personal opinions of this magazine or editors. Some content royalty free. Some content qualifies as fair use under copyright law as use rationale, this being some images & credited quotes, used for critical commentary & discussion of the topics by an educational non-profit organisation. Any other uses of this content may be copyright infringement. All other content © held by Shambhallah Awareness Centre, The Happy Medium Publishing Company & Shé D'Montford 2019 - However views expressed do not represent those of the publisher or associates.

Sarah's ritual for clearing the energies of the previous day and establishing positive boundaries in her shop Earth Spirit. Performed each day

CREATING BOUNDARIES TO PROTECT

One thing that I learnt over the many years working in this industry is we need to protect ourselves. When working with the energies of many people, when we are empaths and healers , we draw people needing energy and needing help . Quite often they will try to take ours, so one of the most important ways of protecting ourselves is to have boundaries. This protects us from giving too much of ourselves to other people, our energy, our time, which in turn can lead to our health being affected.

Knowing when to say NO when working with people is an important place to start. We want to help EVERYONE so much, as this is what we do, we tend to forget about helping ourselves. What use will we be to heal or help anyone if we forget about our own health??? How can we help heal others when we are not healing ourselves? We need to say no when we do not feel in the right place to do a healing. It is ok to take some time out for yourself to rest and heal and connect with nature, as this is an amazing way to heal. Do not feel guilty doing this , as you will be no good to anyone if you do not.

Also you can be picky about who you read for or do healings for. If a client makes you very uncomfortable, then you do not have to book them in with you. If they are constantly draining you of your energy with constant readings etc, it may be time to let them know that they need to do some energy work of their own. Empower themselves by doing some work in their own time and giving your guidance a chance to pan out, as things do not happen over night.

These are all boundaries that will help to protect you and keep you from having issues with these Psychic Vampires down the track. It is ok to say no sometimes, this is how people respect you and know that you have your own inner power and very healthy and strong energy as well.

Put these boundaries in place right from the beginning, or start right now. You will be amazed how protected and empowered it will make you feel.

Feel the magick

Sarah- Fay

CRYSTALS & SYMBOLS FOR PROTECTION

| Crystal Mandala | Moonstone & Lapis Lasuli in a fire triangle | Sarah Fay Invoking Personal Psychic Boundaries | Pentagrams + Gemstones | Labradorite |

Safe in the Arms of the Goddess

PHOTO CREDIT:
Anna Innerstar by
David Russel Smith

A LONG LINE OF INTUITIVE WOMEN

From the 16th century onwards, a seventh daughter was widely thought to have psychic powers, usually as a healer, but sometimes as a dowser, fortune-teller or witch; even more powerful was one whose father (or mother) was also a seventh son (or daughter) The seventh son of the seventh son or the seventh daughter of the seventh daughter is said to possess supernatural powers. In the Tamar a female child born in this way may be high priestess. There were seven planets in ancient astronomy, the world was created in seven days, each of the four phases of the moon lasts for seven days, seven notes on the musical scale, seven colours in the rainbow, seven is the number of wisdom, truth and harmony.

My grandmother was certainly a super intuitive witch who was as eccentric as she was industrious. My Romany Gypsy Grandmother Lillian Ethel Mary Willmott was born in 1914 in Dorset England, born the seventh daughter. As a teen she lived in a convent for 5 years and trained as a nun but left when she was around 20. She never knew about the origins of her gypsy heritage, 5 of her siblings were fair, only one of her other sisters had olive skin, black hair and dark eyes like she did. Rumours surfaced around her mother having an affair with a gypsy during the war, but nothing could ever been proven.

Most witches own familiars, some prefer cats, some prefer dogs or other animals. My grandmother Ethel had a beautiful large black cat named 'Moggy' as her witches familiar. Moggy would follow her everywhere and sleep on her lap and when Ethel dosed off in an arm chair. Many a family member had been frightened to death when both Ethel and Moggy would awake at the exact same moment in bolt upright position when someone entered their space. My familiar is a 47 kg Bullmastiff named Envy. Early memories of my grandmother Ethel, were sitting out in her garden amongst the flowers and herbs. Ethel would make clothes and knit socks and scarfs and then barter the handmade wares in exchange for vegetables at the local market place. Ethel would push an old fashioned pram around with all her shopping in the pram. This pram quite often included me, surrounded and being squashed by cauliflowers and potatoes. Grandmother Ethel, was also kind to the gypsies that used to come around to the door to sell bunches of lucky heather, inviting them in for a cup of tea. Tea leaf reading and tarot were coming practice in her home. My mother Dorothy inherited by grandmother's spiritual gifts, a very intuitive woman with healing hands. I feel very blessed to have intuitive gifts passed down from many generations of woman.

As an Empath, Clairvoyant and witch, I feel and channels energy in an intuitive and heightened way. This energy stream includes other people's feelings alive or dead. I receive images and symbolic messages which allow me insight in to people and places past and present. I have been drawn to helping people for as long as I can remember, which lead me in to working in counselling field for over 15 years supporting numerous people of all ages and beliefs to find their light in times of darkness and uncertainly. Since 2017 I have been working as one of the resident Psychics for Paranormal Projects Gold Coast. We support many private investigations in to the paranormal and offer families insight and closure in the realms of the spirit world. I enjoy incorporating a variety of modalities into my spiritual work: Reiki, Psychometry (reading objects eg: jewellery) Pendulum, dowsing, Tarot, dream interpretation, locator readings and spell casting.

Innerstar – Anna - Spiritual Counsellor - Gold Coast - www.innerstar.com.au

ANNA'S SIMPLE PROTECTION SPELL

What you will need:
- Salt
- Dried basil

1. Mix together 90 % salt to 10% basil,
2. Recite:

Elements of Water, Earth, Air, & Fire

Surround me and my

home with a protective circle.

Whether day or night,

my protection resides

burning so bright.

Bad tidings wished upon me,

Will return to you in 3's..

So mote it be!

3. Sprinkle salt around the inside perimeter of your home and then the outside perimeter.

Earth Spirit Psychic Fair
31st October to 3rd November 2019

Earth Spirit-Natures Clothing & Giftware
Rear 200 Anson St - Orange - NSW - 2800

Ph. 02 6362 9773

http://earthspiritnatures.com.au
https://www.facebook.com/earthspiritshop

THE GATHERING 2018

Steph & Hayley lighting up the room

Rowena Andrews & Michelle Cole

Danielle Redmond doing a great Angelina Jolie impersonation

Your Editor She' D'Montford spreading her wings

Greg the Viking

Mary Lee is right on the mark

Sarah Stephens, Ursula Sonsalla, Greg the Viking, Jacqui Krystal, She' D'Montford

On Nov 22 "The Gathering" dinner for 70 people kicked off the Earth Spirit Psychic Fair with special guests our editor, She' D'Montford, Jacqui Krystal & Ursula Sonsalla at the Duntryleague historic mansion. Everyone danced the night away to live music provided by "Nocturnal." We all stepped into another world of magick, fantasy, myths & legends.

Max Gregory as Sherlock Holmes. Fay Gregory as Mary Poppins

Sarah Stephens as the Elf Queen at The Gathering

Ed Stephens as the Elf king at The Gathering

PHOTO CREDITS: Clayton Rose from CR Photography & Drone Pilot

A HEALING ARTIST

Junko is an Associate Instructor & Member of The Japanese Pastel Hope Art association. She teaches art as a healing, visionary release.

So what are Junko's visions for the future?

"I have plans to make a deck of oracle cards from my art and poems and other possibly publications too .

Junko & her daughter Juli are the practitioners at Shinebow Healing

Junko Kimura's art lives in the rich colours of the altruistic world. Her training In Aura Soma makes her aware of the sacredness of all of the different hues and shades. The colours connect her with the angelic realms from with she channels her artistic visions of a world that harmonises with nature and is free from pain.

In the future I hope to extend Shinebow Health Centre, into a Holistic School focusing on old wisdom, health, sports, music, art and colour,. This would ultimately become a retreat space near the beach with time for healing and relaxation for all.

Supporting the community is important to me. Especially children who do not have support from their parents, so that these children can have a vision for their own future where they feel safe. I have a vision of a safe small village for children in difficult places overseas that would extend humanism around the Earth."

It is about more than massage
Therapeutic Deep Energy Healing
Brings Mind, Body & Spirit
Back into Harmony

PRACTITIONERS:

JUNKO: Aromatherapy & Relaxation Massage Remedial Therapy, Core Myofascial Therapy, Relaxation Aromatherapy, Energy Healing with Reiki & Quantum Touch, Chakra Balance Healing with Colour Therapy

JULI: Remedial Therapy(dip), Myofascial Therapy(Deep Tissue), & Energy Healing with Reiki(Gendai-Reiki Master) & Qumtum Touch(L1)

https://www.facebook.com/shinebowhealing.jk
m.me/shinebowhealing.jk

0413 687 563

Protection Spells

Protect Your Property

Protection is associated with the god Mars/Ares whose day is Tuesday, his colour is red, his herb is tobacco, and his flower is the portulaca. The most basic protection spell would, therefore, be done by assembling the above things on a Tuesday. Light a red candle rubbed with some tobacco and state your request for protection. 63 is the number of the god Mars/Ares, the archetype of protection. Secretly write the number 63 on things you would like protected and say this old invocation: -

Ave Aries

I have been attached to your holy form.

I have been given power by your holy name.

I have acquired your emanation for the goods,

Lord, God of gods, master daimon.

Try supercharging your protection spell by adding the following ancient hermetic phrase to the end of the above chant. Don't worry about the exact pronunciation. The correct phrasing has been lost over time; however, the energy attached to the intention behind these words has continued to build with the passing years and is extremely effective.

"ATHTHOUIN THOUTHOUI TAUANTI LAO APTATO."

The Sator - Rotas

One of the oldest and best known written magick squares is the SATOR/ROTAS Square. You can find the SATOR/ROTAS on walls and vessels of ancient Rome and is still used as a protective charm. This practise was in place in the 1200's when it was found on the wall of the Duorno, Vienna. It was placed there by the builder to protect the church from negative influences. One of the earliest depictions was in Pompeii. (Destroyed 79 A.D.) In amulet form, it can be used as a protection against sorcery, poisonous air, colic, pestilence, early souring of cow's milk, and against rabid dogs in medieval times. This powerful talisman was often used to prevent fires and theft.

The SATOR/ROTAS reads the same, up and down, back to front. The reversing words are SATOR, AREPO, TENET, OPERA, and ROTAS. SATOR and ROTAS are palindromic, as are OPERA and AREPO. TENET crosses itself in the middle of the square, the letter N being the centre of the square, the root holding it all together. The meaning is no great mystery as they are Latin words that you can look up in any Latin/English dictionary: -

- **Sator** = Sower, planter father or promoter.
- **Arepo** = Shortened form of the name of a hill in Athens called "Mars Hill" an open air criminal court; can refer

to person/s from a court. Pertaining to the God Mars/Ares.

- **Tenet** = To hold, keep, restrain, prevail or occupy; has come to mean an ideal held central to a belief system.
- **Opera** = Exertion, work or service, to do ones best; has come to mean a work of drama set to songs.
- **Rotas** = Potter's wheels, torture wheels, car, disc; to rotate. Cycles.

This imputes a request to Aries to exert himself to bring justice to the petitioner on principle and to break a bad cycle or a curse and to turn the wheel to begin a new better cycle.

Protect Your Home

To use the SATOR/ROTAS square for this purpose: - Draw the SATOR/ROTAS on a piece of paper and place under front door mats, on window sills, under mattresses and on gate posts to provide protection for your family

To Protect Pets

Write the SATOR/ROTAS square on a small piece of rice paper and allow your pet to swallow it along with their feed.

The Magick Square of Protection

Not all magickal squares are based on "spelling" only. With the advent of Gematria - letters as numerical values - and a proliferation of magickal scripts, these eventually evolved into numerical form. As with the textual magick squares it can be read each way and adds up to the same value on each line. This square adds up to 63 the number of the god Mars/Ares. To supercharge any protection spell add the magick square of Mars shown: -

11	24	7	20	3
4	12	25	8	16
17	5	13	21	9
10	18	1	14	22
23	6	19	2	15

To Turn Enemies Into Friends

Finally, try this slightly more advanced but highly effective little spell. It uses ancient Greek composite words to invoke the egregore of Mars. Again, don't worry about getting the pronunciation exactly right. You will find that these words have a force of their own. Say: -

TH⊕⊕UTH TH⊕⊕UTH

Restrain the anger and wrath of (NN)

towards me

(NN) *with the authority of the great God*

NE⊕UPH NEI⊕TH

Repeat this three times.

All these protection spells are from Shé D'Montford's book, **"Quick Useful & Effective Spells for the Seven Most Wished For Things"**

Distributed through Ingram and available from all good bookstores or you can order it on-line here:

http://www.lulu.com/shop/sh%C3%A9-dmontford/quick-spells/paperback/product-18874554.html

A WITCH'S HOME

Members of Our Community Invite You Into Their Homes

*Just around the corner
Hiding down the street
There's a curious house
Where magick people meet*

WHAT IS IT LIKE INSIDE A REAL WITCH'S HOUSE ?

Witches and all Magickal folk are very sensitive to their environments. They spend a lot of time making sure it is nourishing and proactive. You will not see the pantomime dark room laden with cobwebs as the habitation of any true magickal practitioner. Their home's reflect their practice of psychic hygiene and a deep connection with nature.

A PROTECTIVE REAL HOBBIT HOLE STYLE HOME

You cant get more connected with nature than living underground with trees growing out through the roof! From the street you'd think Kurt & Deni's home was an empty block but magick is hidden beneath. It brings reality to Witchcraft being an "Underground" movement. Despite being underground, their home is light and airy. The atmosphere is still and peaceful, in contrast to the two vibrant characters who inhabit it. **Please View Phots right.**

Denni & Kurt Live Under Ground in Queensland, Australia

KIMI RAVENSKY'S PROTECTIVE TREE OF LIFE

Kimi says: "Everyone should have a Tree of Life in some form, not necessarily a tree as such, maybe a box , a special shelf, scrap book. Whatever ! It's like a saving of memories of people that have passed through our life, some remain some have come and gone but they have left their IMPRINT! which is safe and saved. My Tree of Life is actually a tree. Started as a dead Bonsai I saved from a friends bin about ten years ago. My friend told her kids if they can look after the tree and keep it alive they can have the pet they wanted. The kids still have not got a pet. But I have a thriving tree, yes it's own life is gone as we know it, but it lives on by the offerings that have been given, offered and sometimes just appear. Everyone that visits my Hobbit House is asked for an offering to put on the tree, I have only ever had one person refuse . My tree has all sorts of things from bling to hair to nail clippings to a tiny broom, earrings baubles even a rather lovely ivory coloured angel and various bags of herbs. This tree lives again and is most certainly alive."

Kimi RavenSky's Magickal Home in Canberra Australia

Kimi's Tree of Life

There's a sense of the sacred and the ancient in the homes of truly magickal people a bit like a temple crossed with a museum

Hidden At Street Level

A Magickal Home Protected Under Ground

...eni walks on the front lawn which is her roof that overlooks her secret garden.

Below ground level their home opens to the sky

Kurt and friend dangling their feet into the back yard

Deni's Altar - What can you see reflected in her Magick Mirror ?

Below Kimi Ravensky performs a ritual in her living room, to invoke love, laughter, healing & friendship into her welcoming home - Photo by Ashley Scott

Photo credit: SASHA ALEXANDER

Celebrity Witch Interview: Fiona Horne

FIONA HORNE SPEAKS EXCLUSIVELY
with Magick Magazine's Editor Shé D'Montford

The 90s was a game changing decade for the craft of the wise in Australia. It was still criminal to be a witch in every state except for NSW. Slowly by slowly we began to force each state government's hand to recognise our religious rights. Lucy Cavendish published "Witchcraft Magazine," the first freely available magazine about the craft written by practitioners of the craft. I became Australia's first "Religious Pagan" marriage celebrant and got the first Pagan church recognised outside of NSW, in Queensland, whilst it was still criminal to practice the craft under Queensland law. The Pagan community started to fight for it rights in court. Through all the turmoil Fiona was out there, showing the way forward, being a very public and very cool face of the craft. She was singing rock-songs about The Goddesses with her band Def FX, she was giving interviews, hanging with hipsters, performing in successful stage plays and was even featured in Playboy magazine. It was revolutionary. It changed the way people pictured the craft in Australia. No longer were witches thought of as ugly, misfit, warty things dressed in black, like bad Hollywood caricatures. Fiona made the media think of us as the cool, fit, attractive, "it" crowd. They put her on reality TV. In "Celebrity Survivor" and she showed that witches thrive in nature because of their deep personal connection with it. They put her in "Mad Mad House" and she showed that witches were the sane influence. Fiona Horne showed Australia and the world that Aussie witches were people you wanted to be around and wanted to know more about. She became both a sky and deep sea diver as well as a commercial pilot, which, as Fiona says, "...is a much more comfortable way to fly than on a broomstick!" Now Fiona has taken it to the next level. She is showing that witches can be a compassionate, vital, connection with humanitarian and animal rescue work.

S: Fiona can you tell us a little about what you have been doing with your aid relief work and what motivated you to begin?

F: Five years ago, I was working on an eco museum conservation project in Baja California (a part of Mexico just a two hour drive south of San Diego) and I was shocked to see children with rotting teeth in the local villages ... so close to a cosmopolitan city like San Diego. I spoke to some local people and they said there was a 'Flying Doctor' service – a small plane that occasionally flew in and landed on a dirt road behind the village and brought a dentist and doctor for the children. The villages were very poor. At the same I was getting my private pilot license and struggling with the amount of study and comprehending the mechanistic world of aviation – I knew I wanted to fly though (I talk about why in my book – it's not the reason you would probably think!) When I saw these kids, it was like a light bulb went on in my brain and I 'prayed' to 'my idea of God/dess' and asked – 'Please help me grasp the knowledge and skills necessary to fly and I will donate my time and skill to aid work to help children and families like these.'

And suddenly, I could remember all the airspace rules, regulations and V speeds and flows and maneuvers and aircraft systems, and comprehend and use the information safely and effectively. And I soon passed my private pilot checkride… and went on to (in 2016) getting my commercial multi engine rating, as well as doing a bush flying course in South Africa to hone my skills to fly aid into stricken and remote regions.

I talk about identifying areas and communities to help and how to go about this in my book, but in a nutshell, I focus on donating my skills to grass roots aid organisations, like the Good Samaritan Foundation of Haiti (GSF) - that do small scale specific aid relief with a view to helping communities rebuild after an environmental disaster, or long periods of political unrest, and become self-sufficient again. My first aid mission that I coordinated and flew was this year (2017) in February, working with the GSF- we flew 350 laying chicks, 100 pounds of long bean seed and building tools plus an agronomist and the director of the Foundation - an amazing woman named Mandy Thody - to Haiti to deliver the aid directly to the island of Ile E Vache that was devastated by Hurricane Matthew last year. The aid we took in is already providing 500 families with daily meals and 270 children's school lunches with egg protein every day. The community gardens are rebuilt and yielding vegetables. The community is growing strong and self-sufficient again.

I am grateful to be a part of efforts like this. I coordinated a second follow up mission in March and am putting a third together for October this year.

On a weekly basis, I fly animal rescue and aid - most recently organizing the travel for two island dogs whose owner died tragically, to the family on the mainland. Last week I organized the delivery of 17 donated crates that allowed 17 dogs to be flown from an island shelter where they were destined to be put to sleep, to loving 'forever homes' on the mainland.

I also work in youth outreach - helping local kids get a taste for aviation, speaking at schools and taking them flying, hoping to inspire them to pursue a positive career as they grow through their school years.

S: How do you feel you have been able to utilize magick to change the world into a better place?

The magick I practice now is a way of life, a way of identifying how to be of service, and how to be the best version of myself so that I can be useful in the world. I don't cast spells like I used to - nor do I encourage others to anymore - with a finite view of 'getting what you want.' I suggest to people that the way to make your 'spells work 100% of the time' is to identify how they can serve others. And then show up to life and do the work, honestly, authentically and sincerely… and then the Universe conspires in your favor and you are taken care of, usually in a way that is better than you could have imagined and tried to conjure.

WITCHES DO FLY!
Fiona Horne is now a commercial pilot who also flies community aid runs for charity.
Below left :Flying Animal Rescue for WHO
Below right: An 'Aid Relief Mission' in Haiti

Fiona Horn in the Def FX days

Image Credit: Tony Mott

S: Monash University did a very interesting study on people who grow to work with the paranormal and a disproportionately high number of them were orphans, adopted and or abused as children. You speak in your book about your sense of isolation at being an adopted child. I understand this as I am adopted too, as are many of our readers. What do you feel it is about these circumstances that draws people to seek an understanding of the greater unseen world we live in?

That does sound very interesting! I would love to read that study! I think that as adopted and/or abused children we have a higher tendency to feel isolated – and this feeling of isolation can become a portal for an introspective view of the world... sometimes for the better and sometimes for the worse...! But it gives us a foundation to view the world 'from outside the norm and the masses' and I think that mindset assists in occult studies and practice.

S: In a nutshell, what different magickal traditions have you studied"?

Gosh, over the last 30 years in varying degrees... Thelemic, Order of the Golden Dawn/ High Magick, Gardnerian and Alexandrian, Dianic... and then I came out of the broom closet as a Witch and decided I was an Eclectic with a Wiccan foundation. Now I am just a Witch... a devout, yoga practicing Witch!

S: Your book has lots of pics of your famous friends. Celebrities are naturally attracted to your lovely aura. I can personally attest to the fact that you are just a lovely person. But magickal people flock together - Do you feel that many celebrities are magickal people?

Lol! I don't know about famous friends so much. They are people whose paths I crossed at times that were pivotal in my life – and that influenced the choices I made and the lessons I learned as I describe in the book.

I appreciate you saying I have a lovely aura! (You do too, She! I look forward to when our paths cross in person again!)

As I talk about in the book, often I clung to the world of 'celebrity' desperately ... trying to survive in a cut-throat town like Los Angeles. I hoped some of their lustre would rub off on me. And yet through all the superficiality, some deep and lasting friendships formed. And I ended up surviving in LA and having a pretty solid career in that industry. I can look back and appreciate it now. But at the time it felt like nothing I did was good enough. I talk about this destructive pattern of thinking and behaving in the book – and how I learned not to be like that anymore. I love going back to LA now to visit as an aviator, a professional pilot, wanting nothing from the entertainment world ... and getting to enjoy its creativity, color and extraordinary characters without any agenda.

Magickal people tend to be creative people – no matter what they do for a living.

S: A beloved mutual friend, Barrington Vincent Sheman, who was an integral part of the AustralianMagickal community and a friend of yours from the early music industry days, passed away recently. Many of our readers miss him. What is your favorite memory of him?

I was scared when I first met Barry! I was so caught up in my own fear of inadequacy. He was the real deal! And behind the wild persona, a deeply magickal and deeply sweet man. May he rest in magickally musical peace.

S: We, here in Australia, miss you. It was so good to hear about your new book and to hear that you have been living a magickal life in the US Virgin Islands, but do you miss Australia?

I am grateful and touched you all remember me! I have lived away from Australia for so long now that 'home sick and missing' feelings have transformed into something else... 'Appreciation' for a vast and beautiful land.

Making A-List friends in Tinseltown with her witchy ways. Fiona Horne at the Australians in Hollywood gathering

I really want to get a small plane and fly off into the Outback! One day! I think my publishers want me in Australia next year for a belated book tour... and maybe a couple of other creative projects! We will see! Right now, I am very focused on my jobs here in the Caribbean, flying, teaching yoga, fire dancing and doing the Aid and Rescue work. But I look forward to being back in Australia one day soon!

S: What is your personal favorite Magickal career highlight?

I think the day it stopped being my career and became just a part of me again.

Having the opportunity to write my autobiography and be back in the public eye again is kind of extraordinary. I did not think this would happen. I was focused on rebuilding my life as a pilot and working aid – after years of being unable to see the light at the end of the tunnel, crawling through it and lighting the bloody thing myself - as I talk about in the book...! And this meant reinventing myself – or maybe more accurately, rebirthing – to arrive at a version of myself that I can be at peace with and happy in the world – and a better, more giving presence. The way I live now is the most magickal I have ever felt.

If you miss Fiona like we do, you can keep up with what she is doing at her official website http://www.fionahorne.com.

Fiona Horne's extraordinary journey through the metaphysical & mundane worlds with all its breathtaking twists, turns & perils, is both heartbreaking & inspirational. She reveals all in her new book
"**The Naked Witch.**"
Grab a copy from any good book retailer. You can also visit Fiona's website to easily order a copy online, print & Kindle/e-book.

DRAGONS BLOOD - The Scent of Protection

Dragons blood, is a resin from the Dracaena cinnabari, the Socotra dragon tree or *dragon blood tree*, is a dragon tree native to the Socotra archipelago, part of Yemen, located in the Arabian Sea. When the tree is cut, the deep red free flowing sap makes it look like the dragon trees are bleeding. Hence its common name. It was also called cinnabar. However, that most often refers to the large, hardened, deep red, resin chunks that were a favourite of ancient Chinese carvers.

Dragons Blood is resinous in more than on sense of the word, because it conducts sound well it has been used as the preferred coating for topped violins for over 2 centuries. Before that it was used as a red dye for wool.

Dragons blood is associated with the element of fire, and the planet Mars. It is very potent and powerful, and can be used for healing, protection and banishing. It is excellent for clearing space, as it drives away negative energy, and in turn can attract what you want to you. It is a perfect ingredient in any form, to protect your property/home and all its inhabitants. Combined with Carnelian, this makes the perfect protective solution.

Angela Roberts

Sensory Energies

Explore our range of divinely inspired soy candles with unique scents or allow the healing energy of reiki to wash over and rejuvenate you in one of our sessions.

Enquire today!
0410 861 728

SensoryEnergies@gmail.com
www.facebook.com/sensoryenergies

THE ART OF PYROGRAPHY

ARTWORK BY ROBYN JOY BLACKFORD

There is more to pyrography than just decorating wood or by burning a design on the surface with a heated metallic point.

A skilled artist gives character to each stroke by applying just the right amount of pressure. The timber is more than just a canvas. Its grain suggests the image and angle and its character becomes part for the finished image which gives it a life that cannot be conveyed in any other medium. It is warm and rich. It embodies the spirits of both earth and fire. It releases a spirit grown in the timber awaiting the artist to become the medium of its emancipation. All this and more is captured in the work of Robyn Joy Blackford. It is a privilege and an honour to have her in our magickal community. Robyn can be contacted on robynjblackford@gmail.com and is available for commissions.

Magick Magazine

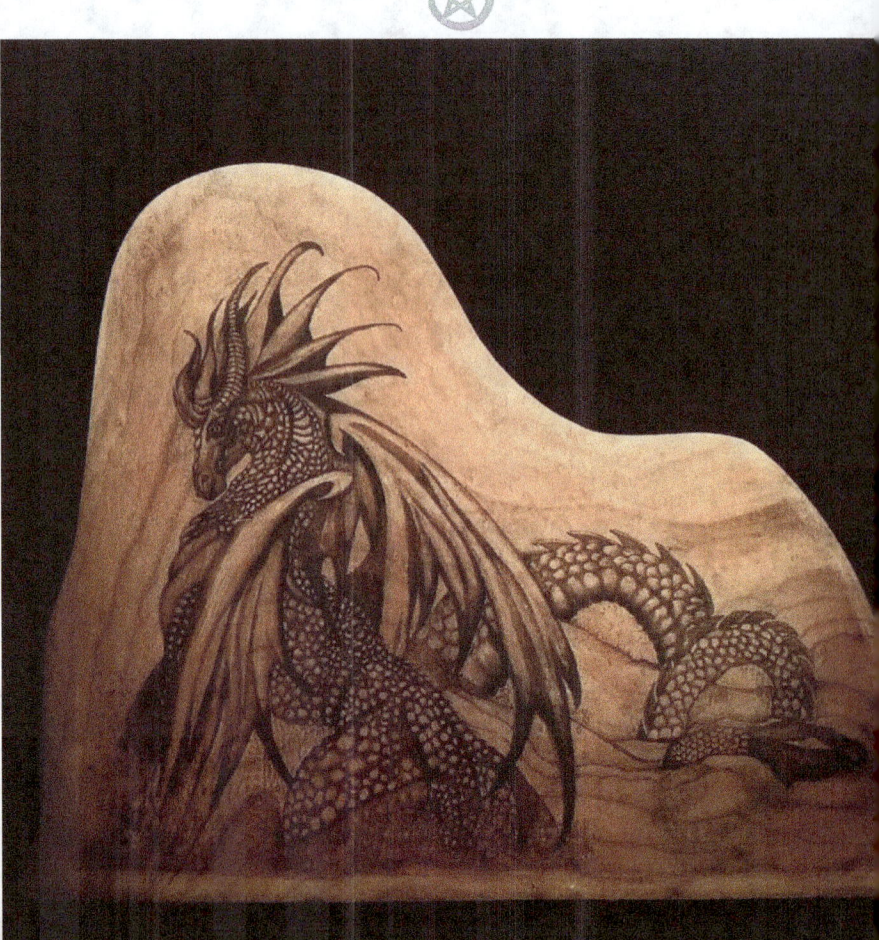

THE WITCHES' MARKET 2018

Magick Magazine No. 8

THE WITCHES GATHERED on November 10. Along with the witches was a cast of amazing shaman & out of this world beings on site to awaken your senses & help you connect with your own intuition. Smells, sights and sounds to transport you to another time. You will find everything a Good White Witch or Dark Witch or Rainbow Coloured Witch needs! There were lucky door prize competitions for anyone wearing a witch's hat, sorts of magical goodies available, crystals, herbs, teas, oils, talismans, knick knacks & more. Drumming Circles, Holistic Healing, Witchy Everything in this jam packed Bewitched Event! Next year you have to dust off your hat & grab your best friend & enjoy a magical afternoon out with these amazing friendly witches & wizards! Children are welcome too. Bringing unique, crazy, open minded people together in an enchanting, bewitching & magical nonjudgmental, drug & alcohol free environment. WWW.MYSTICEVENTS.COM.AU

HERMETIC INVOCATION TO HERMES GOD OF MAGICK

MERCURY

8	58	59	5	4	62	63	1
49	15	14	52	53	11	10	56
41	23	22	44	45	19	18	48
32	34	35	29	25	38	39	28
40	26	27	37	36	30	31	33
17	47	46	20	21	43	42	24
9	55	54	12	13	51	50	16
64	2	3	61	60	6	7	57

Know The God You Are Invoking:-
Mercury/Hermes: Hermes had incredibly humble origins as a god honoured by the shepherds of Arcadia. At the time he was associated with movement, action, the wind, profit (both lawful and unlawful) and games of chance. He later became a patron of travellers, both in this world and the next, where he was a conductor of souls. He was also the messenger of the Gods, a task which he carried out with great diplomacy and tact. He was also associated with learning and mental agility. He was often portrayed as an athletic runner, wearing a round winged hat and winged sandals. He carried the caduceus, symbolising good health and healing.
Colour: Orange.
Sent: Cinnamon
Numbers The numbers associated with Mercury are 8, 64, 260, and 2080. This is because:
- Each row and column of the magic square contains eight numbers.
- The square contains 64 numbers total, ranging from 1 to 64.
- Each row, column and diagonal adds up to 260.
- All of the numbers in the square add up to 2080

In short, Hermes was the god called upon for matters of knowledge, commerce, travel, healing and magick. Little wonder that eventually Hermes became renowned as a master magickian and reputed author of numerous philosophical texts.

The Opening Ritual From the PGM XXXVI. 312 – 20

"Open up for me, open up for me, door; be opened, be opened, door,
Because I am Horus the Great,
ARCHEPHRENEPSOU PHIYRIGX,
Child of Osiris and Isis.
Immediately, immediately; quickly, quickly."
Tr.: R. F. Hock.

The Instruction: From PGM XIII. 7341077
EAST
Stretching out your right hand to the left and your left hand likewise to the left, say "A."
NORTH
Putting forward only your right fist, say "E."
WEST
Extending both hands in front of you, say " Ē."
SOUTH
Holding both on your stomach, say, "I"
EARTH -The point below PAST
Bending over, touching the ends of your toes, say "O."
MID POINT – straing in fornt of you - the here and now (The Point pf power is in the present moment)
Having your hand on your heart, say "Y."
SKY - The Point Above - FUTURE
Having both hands on your head, say "Ō"

"I call on you, eternal and unbegotten, who are one, who alone hold together the whole creation of all things, whom none understands, whom the gods worship, whose name not even the gods can utter. Inspire from your exhalation ruler of the pole, him who is under you; accomplish for me the what ever I request

I call on you as by the voice of the male gods,
IĒŌ OYE ŌĒI YE AŌ EI ŌY AOĒ OYĒ EŌA YĒI ŌEA OĒŌ IEOU AŌ.

I call on you, as by the voice of the female gods,
IAĒ EŌO IOY EĒI ŌA EĒ IĒ AI YO ĒIAY EŌO OYĒE IAŌ ŌAI EOYĒ YŌĒI IŌA

I call on you, as the winds call you.
I call on you, as the dawn."
(Looking toward East say) "A EE ĒĒĒ IIII OOOOO YYYYYY ŌŌŌŌŌŌŌ"
"I call on you as the south."
(Looking to the south say) "I OO YYY ŌŌŌŌ AAAAA EEEEEE ĒĒĒĒĒĒĒ"

"I call on you as the west."
(Standing facing the west, say,) "Ē II OOO YYY ŌŌŌŌŌ AAAAAA EEEEEE"
"I call on you as the north."
(Standing looking toward the north say,) "Ō AA EEE ĒĒĒĒ IIIIII ŌŌŌŌŌŌ YYYYYY"
"I call on you / as the earth."
(Looking toward the earth say,) "E ĒĒ III OOO YYYYY ŌŌŌŌŌŌ AAAAAAA"
I call on you as the sky."
(Looking into the sky say,) "Y ŌŌ AAA EEEE ĒĒĒĒĒ IIIIII OOOOOOO"
I Call on you as the cosmos,
(Looking straight ahead into the middle distance) "O YY ŌŌŌ AAAA EEEEE ĒĒĒĒĒĒ IIIIIII"

Accomplish for me whatever I ask quickly.
I call on your name, the greatest among gods.
I call on you,
IYEYO ŌAEĒ IAŌ AEĒ AI EĒ AĒ IOYŌ EYĒ IEOU AĒŌ ĒI ŌĒI IAĒ IŌOYĒ AYĒ YĒA 1Ō IŌAI IŌAI ŌĒ EE OY 1Ō IAŌ,
the great name.

Become for me lynx, eagle, snake, phoenix, life power, necessity, images of god,
AIŌ IŌY IAO ĒIŌ AA OYI AAAA E IY IŌ OĒ IAŌ AI AŌIĒ OYEŌ AIEĒ IOYE YEIA EIŌ ĒII YY EE ĒĒ ŌAŌĒ

CHECHAMPSIMM CHANGALAS

EEIOY IĒEA OOĒOE seven of the auspicious names

ZŌIŌIĒR ŌMYRYROMROMOS"

"Ē II YY ĒĒ OAOĒ."

Hermes Invocation From: - PDM lxi 63-78

HarThoth whose seven setter names are :-
The first: "THOYTHKH"
The second "LABINOYTHKH."
The third: "PHRĒRKH."
The fourth: "SALBANAKHA."
The fifth: "Falcon"
The sixth: "Ape" (Baboon)
The seventh: "Ibis"

*"Come to me, Thoth, Eldest one, Eldest one of Re, Who went forth from Atum, who was born in the form, from the limb of Atum! Come to me "Thoth" 'heart of Re', 'Tongue of' Tatenen', 'Throat of the one whose name is hidden.' Come to me HEFKAE HEPKA HEBIK NEKHE P KAI! Come to me Lord of Truth who loves Truth who reckons lifetimes who judges Truth, who does Truth! Come to me in your beautiful face in this good night and make answer to me concerning everything about which I am entreating here today, truly without falsehood therein! Come to me in your form of excellent one, in your secret image Come to me and tell me an answer to everything truly without falsehood therein. It is very good!

From PGM XVIIb 123 & PGM V. 370-446
Hermes, God of the world, who're in the heart,
Orbit of Selene, spherical and square,
The founder of the words of speech
Pleader of Justice's cause,
Garbed in a mantle, with winged sandals, turning airy course,
Founder of expressive speech
For he inspires within a short time ...
The allsubduer, Unsubdued, just as may you judge ...
You offer good things to the good,
But grief to those who're worthless.
Dawn comes up for you,
For your swift night draws near.
You lord it o'er the elements: fire, air, water, and earth'
When you became helmsman of all the world;
Beneath Earth's depths you hold the spirits reigns.
And you escort the souls of those you wish,
But some you rouse again.
For you've become the order of the world,
For you cure too, man's every ailment,
Prophet to mortals –
When ever the fateful day arrives again'
Who sends some oracle that's true,
You're said to be the Moirai's thread and Dream divine,
Who send oracles by day and night;
O eye of Helios, O mighty one!
Send me, I pray your form,
And in you own form graciously appear
And graciously render a task for me.
For I'm a pious suppliant,
And so, while I'm asleep,
Send to me your unerring mantic skill."

Closing Rite From the PGM XXXVI. 312 – 20

"Close up for me, Close up for me, door; be locked, be barred, door, until I open you again.
Because I am Horus the Great,
ARCHEPHRENEPSOU PHIYRIGX,
Child of Osiris and Isis.
Immediately, immediately; quickly, quickly."
Tr.: R. F. Hock.

The Instruction: From PGM XIII. 7341077
SKY - The Point Above - FUTURE
Having both hands on your head, say "Ō"
MID POINT - Strand in front of you - the here and now (The Point pf power is in the present moment)
Having your hand on your heart, say "Y."
EARTH - The point below PAST
Bending over, touching the ends of your toes, say "O."
SOUTH
Holding both on your stomach, say, "I"
WEST
Extending both hands in front of you, say " Ē."
NORTH
Putting forward only your right fist, say "E."
EAST
Stretching out your right hand to the left and your left hand likewise to the left, say "A."

© Copyright Rev. Dr. S. D'Montford, Saturday 7th August 1999 Gold Coast. Australia

Magick Magazine No. 8

FAIRYTOPIA 2018

Barb Meynell as Glynda the Good

A Magickal Family Day

Special Guest Amy Hanson

FAIRYUTOPIA with wings, fairy dust & mermaids was truly an enchanted playground!! Fairies, Crystal Alchemists, Unicorns all turned up to this magickal 1/2 day event to enjoy the awesome food, the exquisite, delicate, precious, creative, intriguing, beautiful, music, magical works of art, craft, jewellery, make-up, scents, candles, soaps, potions, charms & goodies you could ever possibly hope for all in one convenient location. The weather was perfect even though it had rained the day before and the day after. Over 1000 fairies turned up to try to break the world record of the most number of fairies in one location. Even though we were pipped at the post by the Kiwis on the same weekend.. there is always next year!

Amazing Costumes

1000 fairies turned up to try to break the world record

Event Organiser Veronica with members of her family

Hundreds of Magickal Market Stalls

There were lots of male fairies

Such Pretty Girls

So Much Colour

So Many Characters

Our Editor She D'Montford as The Bad Fairy

PHOTO CREDITS Above: Ken Wills

Wings Wand & Tutu
Let's set a New World Record !!
Logan Village RSL – Quinzeh Creek Road
Sat 24 August 2019

UP COMING EVENTS
- WIZARDFEST: Sat 6 & Sun 7 JULY 2019
- FAIRYUTOPIA Guinness World Record: Sat 24 Aug 2019

CHECK OUR WEBSITE FOR UPDATES
WWW.MYSTICEVENTS.COM.AU
touch.newage@icloud.com

0459 511 444

PHOTO CREDITS Right Page: Lyn Graham

Event Organiser
Veronica Lorena Heil

MAGICK WILL SET YOU FREE

When Damien Echols was unjustly convicted of murder, the only thing that could free him was magick

On May 6th, 1993 the bodies of three 8-year-old boys, were found dead in the woods in West Memphis. Disregarding the lack of evidence, the focus of the investigation became three small town misfit teenagers, Damien Echols and his friends Jason Baldwin and Jessie Misskelley, Jr. The only crime they committed was that they wore black, listened to metal music and had an interest in Wicca. The small minded Bible Belt community, were convinced of their guilt, despite a dozen witnesses placing them elsewhere at the time of the murders. It was the witch trials all over again. In the end, it was 6 boys who lost their lives that day, 3 murdered, 3 sacrificed to the mob.

The prosecutors led the gullible teenagers into portraying themselves as worse than the were with questions that made them look bad no matter which way they answered them. They were innocent and did not understand the need of trying to paint themselves in the best light. For example after the prosecutor described our young Mr. Echols as 'the ringleader of a satanic group that had murdered the boys in an occult ritual, he then asked Mr. Echols, if he read books by Aleister Crowley, "a noted author in the field of satanic worship," Mr. Echols said no, then added, *"I would have read them if I saw them."* (NB Crowley himself was well documented vehemently denying being a Satanist on several occasions)

Despite this joke of a trial, in 1996, Damien was found guilty of the boys' murders and sent to Death Row. Mr. Baldwin and Mr. Misskelley both received life sentences. They had vocal supporters who drew attention to their plight. Eventually three HBO documentaries drew international attention to the case, which became known as the West Memphis Three. A number of high-profile celebrities such as Johnny Depp and Eddie Vedder threw their weight behind the case, yet the boys were still left to rot as patsies, due to the lack of any other suspects.

The documentary that helped raise awareness of the witch hunt, and helped to free The West Memphis 3 - Damien Echols Centre

Echols as the Magickal Monk in prison & his deterioration after being sent to Supermax with the worst of the worst and being confined to virtual solitary for 23 hours a day

Mr. Echols decided to utilise the routine of prison as a monastic retreat opportunity for magickal study. He began the more complicated High Magick of The Hermetic Order of the Golden Dawn, the 19th-century occult group that counted Crowley, W.B. Yeats, Bram Stoker and Arthur Conan Doyle as members. He began to get results. At first, he questioned whether his rituals were just him playing mental tricks on himself. "Is this really happening or is this just like my imaginary friend? But what else did I have to do all day?" Then he was startled to experience an angelic manifestation. *"I understood why biblical angels always say right off, 'Be not afraid,' and I never questioned it again."*

In 2003, the state transferred Echols to the new supermax unit where inmates were kept in sealed rooms for 23 hours a day. Lorri Davis, Mr. Echols's wife, said. "The supermax sealed them up in tombs." Yet, the discipline of the GD rituals kept Mr. Echols sane in virtual isolation. *"By the last two years, it was all I did. I slept very little. I would just eat and work out and do magick."*

It is a well worn anthropological theory that our ancestors first turned to magick to even the playing field in an unjust world. Magick was used to bring justice then and Damien reminds us that it can do so today too. Damien developed his own magickal style that saved his life. Being so cut off from nature in his solitary confinement, he decided to use strong sense memories to astrally project himself outside into the seasonal sabbats. Additionally, he describes how he and his wife ..."*would dredge up as much energy as we could and program it with the intent of getting me out. Eventually I stopped thinking about the goal, and it became about the joy of doing it."* The return to joy was the key that unlocked his cell door.

This new magickal technique produced a tangible shift. His wife saw a change in him. *"Even the way he carried himself started to change. He got his confidence back. He absolutely came alive."* Then, magickally, a breakthrough. In July 2007, new forensic evidence was presented in the case. A status report stated: *"Although most of the genetic material recovered from the scene was attributable to the victims of the offences, some of it cannot be attributed to either the victims or the defendants."* Given this and the revelation of potential juror misconduct, the West

This is how freedom feels

Memphis Three negotiated a plea bargain with prosecutors. They were released, having served 18 years and 78 days in prison. Mr. Echols went from prison straight to a party thrown by his celebrity supporters.

Post-incarceration syndrome kicked in for Damien. *"I was shattered, broke, devastated,"* The terms of the plea deal meant that he could not claim wrongful conviction compensation. Prison had prematurely aged him. He suffered from arthritis, degenerated eyesight and short-term memory issues, even though he was only in his late 30s.

He had a hard time reading maps and recognising faces. Movies, would switch him off and put him strait to sleep within 5 minutes of commencing watching them. He could not focus. He couldn't do magick for more than a few seconds. He felt the strength of it fade away. *"You know like in 'The Secret' where people try to manifest a parking spot? Something that insignificant was all that I could do."* Even though he had been an avid reader, there were too many distractions for him to make it through a paragraph, he was even frightened to be alone.

Damien Echols finding sacred places in New York

With a lamassu / shedu, an Assyrian protective deity, often depicted as having a human head, the body of a bull. Here at the Metropolitan Museum of Art in New York

Damien wanted to focus on the future, but his public persona revolved around the worst period of his life. *"Without prison, I would've lived the life my parents did — dead end jobs, horrible health, not happy in their lives. Even when I was a kid I always thought, there's got to be more than this. But that was the world I knew."* So to earn money, he and his wife began promoting Damien's books and documentaries about the case. He was successful. "Life After Death" became a New York Times best-seller. There was also "Yours for Eternity: A Love Story on Death Row," a volume of the prison love letters between he and his wife. And his new book "High Magick: A Guide to the Spiritual Practices That Saved My Life on Death Row."

Re-adjustment happened slowly. Over the next several years, he began to explore the city on his own. New York City is a magickal place. He loved places full of powerful energy like the Egyptian altar at the Met, St. John the Divine and Cleopatra's Needle in Central Park. Mr. Echols developed a supportive community based around magick. Now he can do seven and a half hours of magick in one day. His fans are devoted. They see him as an example for how high magick can improve their lives too.

New York Times reporter, Rachel Monroe describes Damien this way: "Mr. Echols addresses large crowds dressed entirely in black and with arcane symbols tattooed on most of his visible skin, he says

"I'm 43 years old and for the first time in my life, I'm actually happy.""

FURTHER READING: https://damienechols.com - https://en.m.wikipedia.org/wiki/West_Memphis_Three - https://www.nytimes.com/2018/09/26/style/damien-echols.html#site-content

Damien with his wife Lori Davis on the right of him, Amy Berg on the far left, and Peter Jackson on the far right at the 2012 Sundance Film Festival. The documentary "West of Memphis" had 11 nominations including **being nominated for an Academy Award**. It won The Women's International Film & Television Showcase Foundation International Visionary Awards.

Damien Echols Teaching Magick
Notice his huge aura captured in this photo
Photo Credit: David Stoupakis

WHAT'S DAIMEN'S MESSAGE FOR US:

"We're feeding all our energy to Instagram and Facebook and TV shows. This energy is vital. And the point of these practices is to turn that energy back inward, to feed our spiritual growth. The point is not enlightenment. What most people think of as enlightenment is a side effect of magick. If you talk about witches now and people think about Instagram, not Satanism, that lowers the danger level. At least, 'it' (what happened to him) is not going to happen to anyone else. Now, I live completely in the present moment. The two things that bring me joy are magick and things that make me laugh. I want to just let everything else go."

Damien Echol's exciting and joyful positivity shines through his books..."my bones began rustling and whispering to me that reality is an outdated concept that has outlived its usefulness..."

Grab a copy of his newest books from any good book retailer - you can also visit Damien's website to easily order a copy online - A Course in High Magic is available through Audible as a talking book.

The stretched letters, designed by Crowley for the front cover of "Konx Om Pax"

KONX OM PAX
The Mysterious Meaning

Konx Om Pax: Essays in Light, is a book of esoteric mystery stories, by Alister Crowley, first published in 1907.

Crowley is without a doubt the most influential writer on the occult and magick in the 20th century. He love his riddles and conundrums that often turned out to be a case of The Emperors New Clothes. i.e. if you don't see anything then there is nothing there. Still these conundrums have become magick equivalent of Zen Koans, to provoke doubt and test a student's progress by driving the student on to greater exploration of the mysteries where they eventually find a profundity where none truly exists. Many admired Crowley's form of riddling the seeker to sort the gullible from the intelligent and copied his methods. Most notably Robert Cochrane, in his formation of his branch of English Wicca called "The 1734 Tradition" that name being a a cryptic and mystical riddle itself. The book name "Konx Om Pax" is just such a case.

Some claim it is a phrase spoken in the Eleusinian Mysteries to bid initiates to depart after having completed the tests for admission to the

degree of epopt (seer). Yet, this phrase, is not immediately intelligible in Greek. It also contains words form, Sanskrit and Latin.
- The first word is Japanese, a homage to the Koan, being 'Kon x' = Crow
- The Second word is Sanskrit - Om = Sound, Word, Silence or Belonging to
- The Third Word is Latin not Greek = Peace

These can be put to gather to make a play on Crowley own name

Crow of peace
Crow word peace
Crow silent peace or alternatively
Crow Secret Sound Of Peace

Remembering that the middle word has all 3 meanings simultaneously does make it a profound or essentially meaningless phrase.

There are a number of more complicated theories that have been advanced as to its origin and meaning.

S. L. MacGregor Mathers claimed it to have been derived from Khabs Am Pekht, which in the Egyptian language means roughly "Light in extension" or "Light rushing out in a single ray", which is used in the Hermetic Order of the Golden Dawn's Vernal and Autumnal Equinox ceremonies.

Dudley Wright also claimed the phrase to be of Egyptian origin, but with the meaning "Watch, and do no evil".

I like this one by Apostolos Touloupas on Sep 23, 2017: *"Konx Om Pax, or Κόγξ ὄμπαξ, as it appears in the dictionary of Hesychius has had people wondering about its meaning. People think it's a mysterious and sacred phrase, while in reality the meaning and the origin of the phrase are quite simple and would disappoint anyone who would like the word to have a super mysterious aura around it. In the dictionary of Hesychius, there's an entry K-3184:*

Greek	Transliteration	Translation
κόγξ· ὁμοίως πάξ· ἐπιφώνημα τετελεσμένοις καὶ τῆς δικαστικῆς ψήφου ἦχος, ὡς ὁ τῆς κλεψύδρας παρά δε Ἀττικοῖς βλοψ.	kónx: omoíos páx: epifónima tetelesménois kaí tís dikastikís psífou íchos, os o tís klepsýdras pará de Attikoís vlops	the same way as the successful and the judiciary vote As for the hourglass, rather than the Gentile.

The word ομοίως was often abbreviated in dictionaries as ομ.,so someone that saw the entry may have confused it and read it as κόγξ· όμπαξ had thought that it was a mysticistic word or something else crazy. The entry basically says that 'konx' is an interjection of the sound that a little stone makes when it falls in an hourglass and that in Attica they also say 'blops' for the same sound. 'Pax' is an interjection for 'silence!' or 'be quiet!'. So, as you can see there's no mystery here, but a dictionary entry that was altered and misinterpreted for something else, resulting in people going crazy over its meaning."

© Shé D'Montford 2019

What is Konx Om Pax About?

- **The Introduction** contains 3 full pages of quotations from sacred texts and sources such as Dante, Catullus, Jesus, Ave from John Dee and Edward Kelley's Enochian and Egyptian hieroglyphs for the Stele of Ankh-f-n-khonsu.

It then has 4 Zen/Tao Te Ching style short stories.

- **The Wake World**: An allegory for the ascent of a magickal practitioner through the Kabbalistic Tree of Life, accompanied by her Holy Guardian Angel. It was originally written by Crowley as a bedtime story for his daughter, Lola Zaza, with Crowley relating himself as the "Fairy Prince." much like Lewis Carroll's Alice's Adventures in Wonderland.
- **Thien Tao**: A parody that casts a Crowley character (Master Kwaw) as a Taoist advisor to the Japanese "Daimio" (daimyō) in a time of crisis. Kwaw advises a course of study in which people shall be taught the antithesis of their natural tendencies: the prostitute to learn chastity, the prude to learn sexual expression, the religious bigot to learn Huxley's materialism, the atheist to learn ceremonial magick.
- **Ali Sloper, or, the Forty Liars**: A play with simple dialogue based on Crowley's conversation with a friend and his wife on Christmas Day. With only two main speakers Crowley satyrizes himself as "Bowley. It contains his essay "Ameth."
- **Stone of the Philosophers Which Is Hidden in the Mountain of Abiegnus**: A satirical philosophical debate between a socialist, a doctor and others, each contributing a poem. Basil Gray is Crowley who offers La Gitana, a love poem.

Protection Magick
Cross Word

IMAGE CREDIT: Royalty Free promotion still for Disney's The Sorcerer's Apprentice staring Jay Baruchel & Nicolas Cage.

Across
- **2.** Protective father god of house and home
- **4.** Psychic Vampire
- **5.** Magickal Dagger
- **8.** The Law of...
- **12.** A type of magic intended to turn away harm or evil influences
- **14.** Protective charm
- **15.** Wishing adversity on another
- **16.** Crossed Sabers - three words
- **18.** Powerful universal clearer
- **19.** Clearing smoke

Down
- **1.** Protective mother Goddess
- **3.** Tungus word for a soul-retriever
- **6.** Protects surfers from sharks and give good waves
- **7.** One who administers substances for healing - 2 words
- **8.** Triple Goddess Symbol
- **9.** Banishing Element
- **10.** Reflected light
- **11.** Roman protective square
- **13.** Water Cleansing
- **17.** Protective Rings

LORDE: "Im Basically A Witch"

Lorde tweet 24.7.2017 *"A witch casting album love spells"*

BUY LORDE'S LATEST ALBUM "MELODRAMA" HERE
HTTPS://LORDE.CO.NZ

MAGICK MAGAZINE

The 20-year-old Gramme Award winning singer, Lorde, told The Daily Telegraph newspaper she isn't 'weirded out' by supernatural beings, ghosts or spirits, because of her love for all things magickal. Lorde even claims to have a 'connection' with the late David Bowie, who passed away in 2016.

See our article on David Bowie and his magick in issue #4

The Art of :BOWIE

Instead of feeling sad about the death of David Bowie, let's pay tribute to his life by looking at his artwork. Bowie's paintings show he knew art and he took a direct hand as an art director in every stage of his creations. He and Iggy Pop left America 'and moved to Berlin in 1976. Berlin gave him the access to new inspirations. Not only did it influence in his songwriting in inspired him to pain franticly. Bowie's love of German Expressionist Art can be seen reflected in his own work

"You aren't dead as long as somebody is thinking about you."

See more Bowie art here :
https://cryptprivategallery.com/david-bowie-paintings

Child on the Stairs in Berlin

Portrait of Mike Garsonp

PURIFICATION OF AUTUMN

Recently I went out for lunch to run some errands and a co-worker asked me how the weather was upon my return. I informed her it was sunny and humid but that it would most probably rain in an hour or so because of the natural signs I was seeing. This co-worker asked me how I knew and I shared that my mother taught me how to read the signs of nature. This was done through various signs perceived through things such as smells, sunset/sunrise colours, clouds, sounds of insects/animals, just to name a few, in order to predict the weather. Due to my mother coming from a farming family in a small rural village this was second nature to her and her family and helped them to be in tune with the seasons. This co-worker nodded in agreed with me and shared that she had been exposed to something similar through her family and within an hour and a half it did indeed rain.

When my mother was teaching me magick as part of my normal everyday life, I didn't realise how much impact it had on me as an individual and how much it would shape my practice. I have vivid memories of the two of us sitting on a beach watching the sunset where she would explain how that particular sunset was signalling the next day's weather - which always came out the way she predicted. A lot of the magick she taught me was in this vein, like when I had my first headache as a child where she took me into the garden and showed me what herbs to pick, to brew a tea in order to get rid of it. We'd be outside watching the full moon and she'd teach me how to sing to it which in hindsight turned out to be a spell/affirmation and although I was always an observant child who dutifully obeyed my mother because we were very close - I just went along with it as I just thought it was normal. I never knew her connection to nature as well as the deep love and practice of spirituality and magick and sharing it with me wasn't the standard for everyone else and so when I gregariously announced that I was going to be a witch when I grew up at the age of 5 after reading "Meg and Mog" I couldn't comprehend the laughter from the other children around me. Suffice to say I did learn the lesson of keeping silent and not speaking about what I learned publicly afterwards unless I was with likeminded people.

I feel when we are more connected to nature and the cycle of things we are more in tune with the magick around us. I've seen more magick performed by locals at a small rural Greek village seasonal festival than in some huge elaborate staged festivals and I ascribe that to the fact that the former was more in tune with nature and the cycle of the seasons. The one seasonal celebration still held in my maternal grandmother's village in autumn is my favourite as it involves jumping over three fires in a row as a way to cleanse the body and soul and bring in health, prosperity and success. It's also a way to mark the end of summer and rid oneself of any evil. After the last harvest occurs in the village, everyone goes down to the fields and collects the stalks of wheat straw and place bundles of them upon the road before their homes, schools, town buildings and even churches. They build three bundles of straw in succession of each other and as the sun sets they are lit and jumped, sung and danced over. Everyone participates and if you take a walk through the streets you can see these fires set up every so often and the best and biggest is always in the town square – the central focal point of the village and where many celebrations occur throughout the year. Some of the boys and men build huge roaring fires and have competitions to see who can jump the highest. The winner of this competition is deemed to have the best luck for the rest of the year. This practice amongst a few others are still happening to this day even if the village population is dwindling their devotion to the old traditions isn't.

This practice held during autumn could possibly have connections to the Hellenic festival of Anastenaria or Nestinarstvo which originated in Northern Greece and Southern Bulgaria where participants walked barefoot through fire (over coals) as part of a celebration in honour of St Helen and Constantine. This tradition is believed to be a mixture of orthodox Christianity mixed with the local pagan celebrations as was the custom for locals to adapt their celebrations to preserve them.

Here in Melbourne, Australia, I can always tell the changes of the season by observing my garden and the creatures who frequent it. Now that we are heading towards autumn my apples are ready to harvest just before summer's end. The smell of the season has changed and the hay fever I've developed in recent years tells me that certain pollens are in abundance therefore certain tree/herbs/flowers are blossoming. Observing the land around me the earth is beginning to slowly withdraw is greenery in favour of the rich brown colours of the earth. The sun is winding down its effect as we are brought close to the darkness of winter. To celebrate this time of year whilst still honouring my Hellenic roots I have developed my own Hellenic autumn ritual which can be performed before a fireplace, fire-pit, oil lamp or even a candle to symbolise cleansing and purification.

Setjataset is a regular writer on Kemetic, Hellenic, Wiccan and occult subjects and has been featured in several books and magazines internationally. She edited her first book, Sekhmet Daughter of the Sun: A Devotional Anthology in Honor of Sekhmet in 2015. Arch Priestess Hierophant in the Fellowship Of Isis (Lyceum of Heka), Hereditary Folk/Hermetic Witch, Initiated Wiccan Priestess, Reiki/Seichim/Sekhem Master, Tarot Councillor (ATA) who has worked professionally as a reader, healer, purveyor of magickal items and teacher of workshops in various metaphysical and occult subjects. For more go to her blog: https://setjataset.wordpress.com
BACKGROUND IMAGE : Astronomical symbol of the Vesta asteroid

AUTUMN FIRE RITUAL TO HESTIA

IMAGE CREDIT:
The Goddess Vesta/Hestia by **Wanda Shipton**
Vesta is the Roman name for the Greek Goddess Hestia
https://www.facebook.com/wandasangelart/

As seen in the book "**The Inner Goddess Workout**"
http://www.lulu.com/shop/sh%C3%A9-dmontford/the-inner-goddess-workout/paperback/product-21905211.html

The Festival of Vesta/Hestia
is held on **May 6** - See The Almanac for more details

- Purify body by showering or washing head, hands and feet.
- Set up shrine with water, wine, salt, bread, olive oil, incense and an oil lamp or candle.
- Light the oil lamp and repeat the below hymn to Hestia:
- Pour libation of wine or water in Hestia's name.
- Make offering of bread and olive oil and light the incense in Hestia's name.
- Spend some time in quiet contemplation and think of what you need to purify in your life. Are there any obstacles which you need to remove or let go? Are there any habits you need to move past? Focus on these and make some changes to your life by actively working on them.
- Thank Hestia and farewell her.

"I make the offer of light to you
Great and Blessed Hestia
Goddess of hearth and home
I offer my shrine for purification
I offer my home for purification
I offer myself for purification
Be welcome with me
Bless me with your love"

© Setjataset

MENTAL POISONING & BLACK MAGIC

In 1937, the first Imperator of the Rosicrucian Order, Dr H Spencer Lewis, wrote a short book called *Mental Poisoning*.[1] I've read it many times over the years to remind myself of the dangers of 'wrong thought' and how devastating our thoughts can be if not well controlled.

Black magic has been part and parcel of belief systems for thousands of years, and still exists in many parts of the world. Does it work? No it doesn't for most of us, but it does for certain people. Don't take my word for it though, read Dr Lewis' book. So many people scoff at the superstitions associated with black magic when, according to Dr Lewis' book at least, we are actually invoking this power constantly ourselves without even being aware of it.

Okay, so we don't use powders, potions and incantations to deliberately bewitch others, but so many people, through the harmful thoughts they harbour about themselves or others, accomplish many of the harmful things one typically would ascribe to witchcraft. And the worst is that they aren't even aware they're doing it! They aren't even aware that anything untoward is happening.

Mind Power and Suggestion

The mind has a certain 'mind power', it can influence things of a physical nature and at the very least has the potential of telepathically influencing the thoughts and opinions of others. Every time we use the mind consciously or subconsciously to convince anyone of anything against his or her will, and especially when we harbour malicious thoughts about a person, we are in effect doing what practitioners of black magic do, or try to do. At the bare-bones level, this is precisely the process involved in black magic, except that the black magician does it willingly, maliciously and knowing full well what the intended consequences for the poor victim should be.

Black magic is nothing more or less than the acquisition of results through mental suggestion, whether done directly or indirectly, close-up or at a distance, through verbal or telepathic suggestion. In essence, the only power a wizard or witch has, is a highly developed ability to implant fears in the mind of the victim, whether through actions, words or the focused telepathic ability to implant thoughts and emotions in the minds of others. With the intention of harming the other person, the black magician attempts to plant fear and panic in the mind the victim, and hold that fear, panic and blind faith in place for as long as it takes for the poor victim to accept the harmful suggestions being sent. The rest is up to nature, for any firmly held belief is acted upon by the body eventually. With a slick-talking salesperson, the pressure is on for customers to buy things they don't want. It doesn't take much to see the similarity between such pressuring and 'black magic', for it is an attempted imposition on the minds of customers to change the way they think for a brief moment so they agree to buy something they neither need nor want. And even if we think we are trying to sell something 'good' to the customer, are we really qualified to say whether or not the customer needs the things we believe are so 'good'? Parents convince their children that 'bad things' will befall them if they don't behave a certain way, thereby planting fears in their minds. Ministers tell us we'll go to hell if we don't do as the church tells us to. And when a doctor tells a patient death is only six months away, this almost seems to follow, though the patient does not necessarily need to die if he or she had the will to live. And now and then an extraordinary patient proves this to be true. It is what one believes that counts. Similarly, some indigenous people may believe that a certain witch doctor can curse them to death, the suggestion is taken, and sure enough, they die.

IMAGE CREDIT
Autumn Trees - Infrared Photography
Tarek v. Bergmann
ceirtdruid@gmail.com .
https://www.ephotozine.com/user/ly426-95967

We condone negative talks about war, disease, distrust, poverty and so on, which travels around like snowballs gathering in momentum and size with tremendous speed. When we believe in and stoutly proclaim and spread an idea, we help to bring it to pass. We laugh at the fears and naiveté of people in some parts of the world when they believe they have been 'cursed' by a witch doctor. Yet aren't we as gullible in other respects when suggestions are made in a sufficiently convincing manner? Look at how easily a good orator can sway an audience through words alone to do the most awful things. (Trump is a good example). Call it a mob egregore, popular convictions, mass delusion, or whatever, but it all starts with someone implanting a thought, and others then reinforcing it through blind acceptance. All manner of evil has been created in such dramatic ways.

Thoughts Find Their Mark

Whether aware of it or not, we are constantly trying to influence the minds of others to suit our preferences. It may be the 'natural' thing to do, but that does not make it okay, and it certainly leaves its mark karmically on us all. But our kind of 'hidden' black magic goes even deeper than that. Like the witches and wizards of yore, we don't even have to be in the presence of our 'victims' to get results. Whenever we send a harmful thought to someone, we are guilty of the age-old crime of witchcraft. The only difference is that the wizards and witches know what they are doing while we *maybe* are ignorant of our powers. Black magic is based solely upon belief, and if recipients know that evil can come their way but that they do not have to accept it, that they alone have control of their minds, no evil can affect them. But few people realise this and the evil thoughts sent in their direction do affect them. Every thought you send out with feeling lands on its mark, and has consequences. And in all cases, it 'infects' you as much as your poor 'victim', in fact usually a lot more than the person you are thinking badly of. You are in a very real sense 'bewitching' yourself too. Dr Lewis called this *'mental poisoning'*, and there is hardly a better expression to describe the effects. Most people are mild, unknowing, and almost kind witches and wizards. They don't know their own power, or the harm they are causing, and for that reason the consequences are not as severe as they are with people who knowingly engage in such practices. The effects we undergo may be feeling a bit down, feeling sad perhaps, becoming a bit less organised, getting into an argument with someone we would otherwise not have, etc. Wishing a person a bit of 'bad luck' may seem an innocent enough thing, but it has consequences for us, you can be absolutely sure of that. Without the faintest realisation that our thoughts not only affect the people we are thinking of (even if only minutely), we suffer the consequences too.

How do we stop practising black magic and how do we protect ourselves from the black magic sent out by other minds? Control of our thoughts and words is the key. We cannot think bad thoughts and at the same time get good results. Like begets like, always! Whether *thinking* about planting pumpkins or *actually* planting them, remember that it is your thoughts that that initiate everything, and often affect everyone within your karmic proximity. That may amount to quite a few innocent people, and then you wonder why no one likes you!

Stop your Black Magic

So, how do stop ourselves from using 'black magic'? You can't go wrong by beginning to hold only good, positive, uplifting thoughts about yourself, your neighbours, your work colleagues, and the whole world. Do this, and you will stop bewitching yourself and others, and help to control the practice of black magic everywhere. Using the power of our thoughts to raise the moral and spiritual level of thoughts worldwide is after all the greatest thing we could do for our suffering world.

Stopping your 'mental poisoning', stops the black magic associated with it. Both are two-way streets and once started, the one feeds off the other until there's nothing more the feed on. We are all like broadcasting and receiving stations, sending out and receiving thoughts, and of course words. Minds on the same mental and spiritual level constantly contact each other. We all know about mental telepathy and how distance makes no difference. Therefore, to control black magic we must control our own thinking, and send out only good thoughts and receive only good thoughts too.

As we think good, and only good, we grow in understanding and move higher up the scale of thinking. And when you think only charitably of everyone, you build a safeguard against the harmful thoughts directed at you by others. By sending good thoughts into the world, we help lift our neighbours' thoughts, which in turn come back to us as positive and uplifting experiences for a change. If we are habitually negative thinkers, it will of course take some doing to break the habit of negative thinking. If we feel badly about someone or something it is not easy to stop thinking unkind thoughts and turn on the kind ones. Yet if we discover that a certain food (even our favourite dish) causes us discomfort, of course we must stop eating it. It is easier to control our physical habits than our mental ones, but we do have control them both. Once we realise that our ulcers are the result of the arguments we constantly get into, the hurt feelings we are prone to resort to when stressed, and the sarcastic and malicious thoughts we harbour about certain individuals, we know we have a toxic brew in our minds and need to take strong corrective action to turn things around.

Once you begin holding only good thoughts about yourself, your neighbours and the whole world, you will stop mentally poisoning yourself and others, and the practice of black magic will be once step closer to extinction. And isn't learning to use our thoughts to raise the world rather than pull it down really something worthwhile? Of course it is. Be vigilant, watch your thoughts!

by Eli Gilmore SRC, Rosicrucian Order AMORC

The book *Mental Poisoning* by Dr H Spencer Lewis is available as a digital download from www.amorc.org.au/rosicrucianbooks

PLUG INTO THE POWER OF THE UNIVERSE

For over 100 years, the Rosicrucian Order has made available its successful system of personal, home based study that gives you access to the fullest potential of being – physical, mental, psychic and spiritual. In simple weekly lessons you will find that our comprehensive approach makes your learning and personal development process easy.

We invite you to join with us and become part of a worldwide group of men and women dedicated to mystical knowledge in the widest sense.

You can harness virtually unlimited powers of insight, creativity, spirituality. You can attract people and events into your life, speed your body's natural healing processes, create harmony around you. And much more. All you have to do is learn how.

As the first step in discovering just how extraordinary you really are we invite you to read our free introductory booklet *MASTERY OF LIFE* – see it at: www.amorc.org.au or ask for your free no obligation copy by phoning: 1300 88 11 35 or email: mastery@amorc.org.au

AMORC

THE ROSICRUCIAN ORDER

THE ROSICRUCIAN ORDER IS NON-PROFIT, NON-RELIGIOUS, NON-POLITICAL

DO YOU KNOW THE NAME OF
THE WOMAN WHO DISCOVERED WHAT THE UNIVERSE IS MADE OF ?

'Every high school student knows that Isaac Newton discovered gravity, that Charles Darwin theorised evolution and that Albert Einstein came up with the concept of the relativity of time. But when it comes to the composition of our universe, the textbooks simply say that the most abundant atom in the universe is hydrogen. And no one ever wonders how we know. Since her death in 1979, she has not so much as received a memorial plaque. Her newspaper obituaries do not mention her greatest discovery.' — Jeremy Knowles - Dean of the Harvard University

Her name is CECILIA PAYNE.
Nothing justifies the complete lack of recognition for her revolutionary discovery.

Cecila Payne (May 10, 1900 –December 7, 1979) was a woman before her time. Her mother refused to spend money on her college education, so she won a scholarship to Cambridge. However, when Cecilia had completed, Cambridge wouldn't give her a degree because she was a woman, so she moved to the United States to work at Harvard. Cecilia was the first person ever to earn a Ph.D. in astronomy from Radcliffe College, with what Otto Strauve called "the most brilliant Ph.D. thesis ever written in astronomy." You can read her thesis here: http://adsabs.harvard.edu/full/1926PASP...38...33M

Cecilia Payne was the first woman to be promoted to full professor from within Harvard, and is often credited with breaking the glass ceiling for women in the Harvard science department and in astronomy, as well as inspiring entire generations of women to take up science.

Cecelia proposed in her 1925 doctoral thesis, that stars were composed primarily of hydrogen and helium. Her groundbreaking conclusion was initially rejected because it contradicted the prevailing theory of the time, which held that there were no significant elemental differences between the Sun and Earth. Henry Norris Russell, is usually given credit for discovering the sun's composition, however, he came to his conclusions four years later than Payne, after advising her not to publish. Cecilia is the reason we know about stars whose brightness fluctuates. Every other study on variable stars is based on her work.

Cecilia Payne is awesome and everyone should know her.

Matthew Gardner

Book Review:
THE RED GODDESS BY PETER GREY

Do what thou will shall be the whole of the Law.

As most people are aware, Babalon is an extremely important Thelemic deity, who has been treated very badly throughout the ages and whose feminine power has been trampled underfoot by many people and institutions during the intervening centuries.

Peter Grey has written a "history" devoted to the archetype of the divine feminine, Babalon, raising Her to Her rightful place in our modern world and life. It is not a dusty old tome but a rollicking ride through the centuries. The book is only 229 pages long with an extensive Bibliography of particular note.

Peter outlines Her place, or displacement really, throughout the course of history. He takes the reader from the temples of Rome to the Ishtar Gate into Babylon, where She is reviled by the exiled Jews, and to the streets of Jerusalem, where She really had no chance with the rise of Christianity. Also discussed are the visions of St John of Patmos, which are found in the Book of Revelations in The Bible. I believe anyone reading The Red Goddess would benefit from reading these visions John had of Babalon. Poor old John was completely overwhelmed by what he saw.

Peter Grey then discusses the relationship of Simon Magus, John Dee and Edward Kelley, Crowley and Jack Parsons with Babalon and the workings and writings resulting from their relationship. I would recommend reading the beautiful "Daughter of Fortitude" transmission received by Kelly during one of the scrying sessions with John Dee. Babalon in our modern world is discussed and the myriad ways She is in plain view, if we care to look, and how She remains invisible to those who do not see.

She is everywhere – from the red roses in your garden, the red lipstick seen each day as we go about our work, to each glass of wine and flashing neon signs in the red-light districts in each city.

As you can probably feel, I love this book and the cover photo hangs on my wall. I have read The Red Goddess three times, each time learning and understanding more about the importance of the divine feminine in our world. I have my own bespoke bound version of the book, that's how much I believe the message it contains is worth honouring.

Hopefully this short introduction may have piqued your interest enough to read this book or at least, to go look at the cover.

If you joined OTO for the sex Magick, like I did, reading the Red Goddess will go a long way in helping you understand an important pillar of Thelemic Magick.

Love is the law, love under will.

Soror Levanah

MAGICK

It is our aim to make this the best and most reliable resource for Magickal information internationally

Magick Magazine is a unique magazine for the magickal community

Its writers, artists, editors, marketing managers advertisers and production crew are all well respected members of the community.

There are no muggles or unethical people involved in this work.

The magazine will be posted on line in a flipbook format or you can order a full colour softcover book for $12.95 plus postage.

ADVERTISING RATES

Full Page		
A	Dimensions 277mm (H) x 190mm (W)	$800
Half Page		
B	Dimensions 135mm (H) x 190mm (W)	$400
Quarter Page		
C	Dimensions 135mm (H) x 93mm (W)	$200
One-eighth Page		
D	Dimensions 65mm (H) x 93mm (W)	$100
Banner Page		
E	Dimensions 30mm (H) x 190mm (W)	$120
Classied Display advert		
F	Dimensions 30mm (H) x 44.5mm (W)	$50
Classied Line advert		
G	3 lines or 30 words.	$30

VIEW ONLINE AT http://www.magick.org.au

Conditions of advertising: All prices include artwork design

Julie Mason
✆ +61402 793 604

email: julie.mason@magick.org.au

The WEEKLY Seer

The tragic remains of the unfortunate trio

THREE WITCHES DIE IN SUDDEN SHOWER

In a tragic event this week three witches were caught without umbrellas in the driveway of a local community centre, when a sudden downpour came out of nowhere and melted them.

Forensic scientists working at the scene are attempting to identify the victims, but are faced with a daunting task, due to the fact that all three witches have flowed into one puddle, making the job of separating their individual DNA almost impossible.

A spokesman for the police said, "At the moment we are trying to ascertain which witches are missing and then we can start to narrow down the possible identities of the victims. We are, therefore, calling on members of the public to let us know if any witches of their acquaintance have disappeared – other than in a normal disappearing spell, that is."

The witchcraft rain-safety group Weather Event Troubleshooter said that if only witches would check with them before going out, there would be a lot fewer incidents such as this,

As evening approached a forensic team was seen bringing specialist equipment in the form of sponges, mops and buckets to the scene of the tragedy, as they prepared to take the remains of the unknown witches back to the laboratory for further testing.

Morganna with her warm humour is a well respected elder of our community. You can contact her on morganna13@hotmail.com

*The Awakening Imbolc Brisbane Witches Masquerade Ball Theme
EARTH WARRIOR
Dress as your Favourite creature, as we dedicate this magical night to our brothers and sisters of the earth.*

contact Amy on 0428 418 097
email: mysticharmony@hotmail.com

THE BEST LUNA TIME TO CUT YOUR HAIR

If you want your hair to grow faster and have strong roots then cut and feed it during the waxing Moon.

If you want to slow your hair growth and to strengthen hair-roots cut it during the waning Moon.

You may weaken your body if you cut your hair during the new Moon or during a Lunar or Solar eclipse.

The best time for hair-cut is the Full Moon especially when the moon is in your solar birth sign - or the moon phase of zodiac sing that the moon was in when your were borne.

This only happens once a year so be ready for you luna birthday treat

N.B. *Don't Cut Or Treat Your Hair during a Void Of Course Moon* or you may get unwanted results

NOSTRADAMUS' PROPHECIES

The humorous cover of an almanac depicting Nostradamus. 1855

Nostradamus, born in France, 1503, is undoubtedly the most famous 'seer' the world has ever known. His books have almost never been out of print since 1555. The most famous is 'Les Propheties' is a collection of about 1000 poetic undated quatrains. His almanacs contained at least 6338 prophecies.

Catherine Medici, wife of King Henry II of France, commissioned Nostradamus to Paris to draw horoscopes for her family. She was so impressed by him that he became physician and counsel to her son, who would become Charles the 9th of France. Nostradamus had a great deal of influence with in the royal family. He spent years building around himself an orb of mystery. He claimed that dangers in his own time (He believed what he was doing was against religious orders,) caused him to write in enigmatic sentences that he called 'clouded obscurity'. He mixed languages, ancient Greek, Italian, Latin, and played word games in his writings supposedly to avoid detection by the inquisition. However, he would have had to practice Magick to have been outside of the law. Prophecy and astrology were permitted at the time. There has never been found a code, decipher or algorithm or hidden secret to clarify the writings.

Very few predictions were of his own creation. Copy Write did not exist in the 1500's, and Nostradamus freely used passages from Suetonius' The twelve Caesars, Livy and Plutarach. He also copied work from Geoffrey of Vilehardouin, Jean Froissart and Richard Roussat. Who you might ask? Exactly! Nostradamus had the name and the fame to carry it off. Nostradamus himself often claimed that he was not psychic. Even his book title has been mistranslated. It should read 'The prophecies BY Nostradamus, not 'OF.' Nostradamus has been credited with predicting the rise of Hitler, Terrorist attacks, the nuclear destruction of Nagasaki and Hiroshima just to name a few of his favourite disasters. Even in WW2 the Nazis spread propaganda that Nostradamus had predicted Hitler's rise. In response, the allies retaliated that Nostradamus had also predicted Hitler's downfall and death!

Some believe that his quatrains are predicting our own immediate future, for example the fall of technology, the destruction of mankind as we know it and the 3rd world war (which apparently started last year, I missed that one). We are not pointing fingers here at Magick Magazine... we know how deadlines can whoosh past so easily!

Does this mean that we about to enter the most cataclysmic era in the history of the world, or are we reading into this what we want to see through our own biases? Let's face it, nothing grabs our attention more than fear, and mainstream media is all about stirring that up. It is said that the words are so vague, almost anything can be claimed. It is easy task to take undated ramblings and fit them to any event in time, and remain open to interpretation in every generation.Even the translations are unreliable because the English translations did not take into account the meanings of words or phrases from 16th century France. Just for fun, lets have a look at some of the quatrains and their interpretations according to Joolz:

Century 1, Quatrain 87

Volcanic fire from the centre of the earth, will cause trembling around the new city" Two great rocks will make war for a long time. Then Arethusa will redden a new river.
Has been interpreted to terrorist will fly planes into the twin towers on September 11, 2001 in New York City. I personally think that is a bit of a stretch, so here is my own interpretation... Nostradamus was firstly a physician, so I think he is talking about health and food. Centre of the Earth - our bellies, hunger makes us tremble. Two great rocks - bread rolls. White vs Wholemeal, we have been at war over that one for a long time. Arethusa was a nymph from mythology who changed into a fountain. Fountain makes tomato sauce. Red River! See, it is all coming together. Add a sausage and we will be in a happy place. Does anyone know of a quatrain about sausages?

Century 1. Quatrain 25

Lost and found again after many centuries, Pasteur will be honoured a demi-god, When the moon complete her great cycle, He will be dishonoured by another ancient wind.
This one was believed to be about Louis Pasteur. I think there was a spelling mistake and it was meant to read 'pasta'. Nostradamus travelled to Italy and discovered the joys of eating pasta there. Remember back when healthy diets were all about carb loading? Now that theory has been dishonoured and we are all back to high protein and Keto diets.

Century 1. Quatrain 32

The great empire will soon change place, For a better place, it will grow in size, Very tiny place of a small account, In the middle of it, he will lay down his scepter.
This one is easy, he is talking about the Burger King franchise.

No prophesy has been interpreted and proven specifically before the event with the exception of his last one: on July 1, 1556, he told his secretary she would not find him alive at sunrise. He got that one right.

Joolz asks: *Please go to our Magick Magazine Facebook page to debate this or submit any interpretations of your own! https://www.facebook.com/MagickMagazine*

Joolz is our wonderfully cheeky & magickal advertising executive. She keeps our spirits up as we plunge headlong into the craziness that is necessary to produce this magazine for you. Her inspirational ideas have worked magick for many business. Have a chat to her & see if you can get her to work her success spells for you too.
You can contact her on julie.mason@magick.org.au

TASSEOGRAPHY

The art of reading Tea leaves or Coffee grounds is known as "Tasseography"

It started long ago in the days before tea and coffee were even around. It goes back to the times of an Ancient Greek practice, looking at the patterns and symbols made by wine sediments left in the bottom of the barrel, it was a popular method in a culture that revered omens and symbols. In largely non-literate societies, visual symbols play the role of storyteller, seer, guide and counsellor. By the mid-nineteenth century, this form of fortune-telling was well established all over Europe and the Middle East. Gypsies practiced tea leaf reading after tea arrived in Europe early in the 17th Century. Eventually over time, the practice spread all over the world.

After World War ll, it became so popular that women exploring their intuitive side, where regularly reading tea leaves with each other and for their families. Small fortune telling tearooms became a trend, like the old Rendezvous Tearoom that was located upstairs in the Brisbane Arcade, The Rainbow Room, The Mystic Inn, The Gemini Tearoom, The Tropical Inn and The Boston Teahouse. In those days it was illegal to do fortune telling as the laws classified it as a form of witchcraft. The only way for these rooms to survive was to have signs saying: *"We are here as mere entertainers and do not profess to tell fortunes."*

These tearooms were always tucked away like hidden gems and you had to rely on word of mouth to find them. They were always busy little hideouts and you would have to take a number and wait your turn, and yes, they had Police raids. The laws didn't change until around 2001, however, most of these tearooms vanished overtime due to high rents and changing times. It is just starting to become popular again.

To see a PEGASUS in your tea cup means: Olympic endeavours, great success. Your guiding light. Power. Stability. Aspiring to the greatest heights of accomplishment. Being able to harness magic in the material plane. Clear mental focus. Transforming our life in magical ways. Rising above a problem.

The pictures and symbols in the cup reflect the hopes, dreams and concerns of the person who consults this divination. Identifying them and putting meaning to them requires imagination, intuition and practice.

This is my way of doing Mediumship. Quite often I will get messages from past loved ones in the cup. I might be given the initials of the person or be shown an object they loved or use to wear or period clothing. Different types of hats that represented the type of work they use to do or services they were in. What war they were in. Anything that is going to connect to them. I love reading the tea leaves as I can show the person what I am seeing and how is it is to do this for yourself.

Next time you have a cup of tea, try it yourself.
Kate Denning

Kate Denning is a modern day mystic & talented clairvoyant. Kate is highly skilled in the ancient art of Tea Leaf Reading, as well as Palmistry and Crystal Ball Reading. Kate offers one -one one readings, psychic parties, workshops, and live talks.
www.thespiritualrealm.com.au

MAGIC IS 'ALL' AROUND

How to find & use Magic every day

People think magic is something that we need to conjure or have a mystical talent to uncover. A lot of time and energy is spent on acquiring just the right mystics and healers, obtaining readings, crystals, herbs and so on. Being Psychic is definitely a gift to treasure but did you know that every person on the planet can see and use Magic every single day?

What does it look like?

You may not remember it but you have already experienced and created magic. We find magic in the most unlikely of places like; the wisdom within a young child's eyes, the glistening light on a gumleaf, a dog's smile, a whisp of curling fog, the feel of snow flakes on your upturned face. These are all examples of magic and they **are all around you.** You can create and nurture them. All you need to do is to be open, unguarded, observant and present in the moment.

How you can tap into magic?

The simplest way to discover magic is to be still for a moment. All this takes is a few breaths with eyes closed or unfocused gently on the horizon. Take 3 slow deep breaths and relax your body. Now refocus/open your eyes and look around you. Pay attention to the smallest details surrounding you.

Notice the ants, the breeze, the quality of the light as it hits the pebbles at your feet. Now breathe deeply and feel the energy and light fill and nurture your entire body from your feet, to your head and then overflow your being as it spreads into your surroundings. You are now connected to the magic of existence, the earth, the universal light and everything that connects and sustains us.

Practice this regularly and you will find that magic will expand within you. Magic can be found in the heart and soul. This one simple technique connects your mind to the magic within. Expanding your natural abilities is a matter of knowledge, practice, determination and pure wonder and curiosity about the magic you hold. Anyone can draw it out of them and use it daily to the advantage of themselves and the world.

You will know that you've mastered this first step when you start to notice new events and serendipity emerging in your daily life.

How to experience more magic?

Once you have mastered the breathing technique above, you can increase your skills by focussed practice. The next few steps in your magical mystery tour are to:

1. Connect yourself regularly to the planet (Gaia) by meditating (minimum 5 minutes) and expanding your sense of self downward to connect with our planet. Imagine you can reach downward via a golden thread, to touch the planet underneath the building you are in. Allow this touch to move into the planet, where you are welcomed by Gaia with open loving arms. Connect with her and ask her to heal, help and guide you as you re-energise yourself. Gift her anything that is a bothering you right now. Gaia will take everything you don't want and recycle it to renew the planet. Once you have connected to the Earth for a few moments, gently thank Gaia and withdraw the golden thread connection back into your body. Slowly stretch and open your eyes.

2. Repeat the above process but this time open your Third Eye or Brow (Ajna) Chakra and reach the golden thread outward from the top of your head or Crown Charkra (Sahasrara), through the sky, the stratosphere and outward into the Universe; seeking and finding the Eternal Light. Allow the light to rejuvenate your wisdom, strength and soul. Again, spend a few moments there and after thanking the light; return to your body. Finally, slowly stretch and open your eyes.

3. Over time you will learn a lot from what you discover about yourself and your connection to magic. You may discover you are more peaceful, that your intuition increases, you begin to sense things more easily or that you are generally more relaxed and so able to handle the stresses of life more effectively. Whatever the results, honour them and yourself by keeping a Magic Discovery Journal.

When the steps above are done regularly, you will begin to emerge from the human brain 3d world into the magical realm of mystics, psychics and spiritualism. Once you begin, your world will continue to grow and expand along with your

If you'd like to know more about Toni-Maree you can find her at www.toni-maree.com.au While you're there, you might like to discover details of her upcoming "**Psychic Development**" and "**Happiness GPS**" programs.

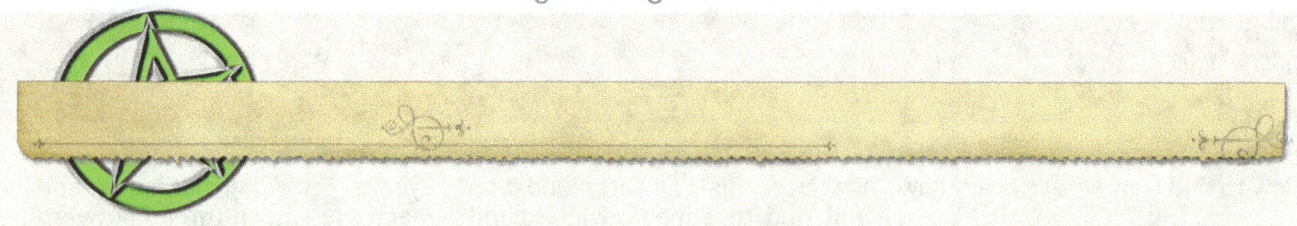

CALLING ALL MAGICKAL EMPATHS

BY RAVEN DIGITALIS

Magick and emotion go hand-in-hand. Emotion fuels our work and fuels our connection to nature, the ancestors, and the gods. A great many Witches and magickal folks identify as empaths. Empaths are individuals who experience empathy at a higher rate than what is considered ordinary.

Though interpretations of empathy may be numerous, the essence remains the same through and through: empathy is the experience of emotionally mirroring or absorbing surrounding emotions. Additionally, and most importantly, the experience of empathy requires a response of compassion. Sympathy, on the other hand, can be explained as "feeling for" a person, whereas empathy is more emotionally intimate and could be described as "feeling as" an external emotion. Empaths are individuals who consistently absorb emotional energy and are no stranger to "walking in someone else's shoes."

I feel lucky to have recently contributed to the ever-growing empathic field with my new book on Llewellyn Publications, called Esoteric Empathy: A Magickal & Metaphysical Guide to Emotional Sensitivity. It is the first book of its type: one where empathy is explored in a magickal and occult lens – however, the science of empathy is not neglected! If you are a magickal practitioner and self-identifying empath, the book was written just for you.

Perhaps over time you've come to realize that you're an empath. You're likely familiar with empathy's pros and cons; its ups and downs. For people who are extremely emotionally sensitive, especially to the point of absorbing external emotional energy on a daily basis, it can be a daunting task to discover methods of personal balance. But empathy is not a curse. It is a driving force of social unity, of instigating love, and of helping heal the world. In order to properly help, empaths must be in a state of balance themselves. For the magically inclined empath, these suggestions may be especially relevant for managing strong levels of empathy on life's journey.

Regular Protection – Rather than choosing perpetual self-isolation, which is a destructively easy response to empathic overload, choose to protect yourself. Consider constructing shields around yourself through ritualistic visualization on a daily or weekly basis. Keep in mind that empaths are notoriously emotionally vulnerable, so if a challenging social situation feels like it has compromised your shields, remember that they can be easily reconstructed with additional visualization.

Daily Spiritual Practice – Life itself is the greatest ritual of them all. We must consciously choose to manage our emotions and personal energies on a daily basis. Rather than getting swept up in life's tedious daily cycles, take some time out for morning and evening prayer, meditation, ritual, and simple quietude. Start in small increments of time and work up to longer periods of practice.

Good Environment – Surround yourself with kindhearted individuals who empower your strengths, encourage your happiness, and positively challenge your perception. Naturally, choose to do the same for them! Don't forget to take breaks when needed; some amount of alone time is deeply beneficial for every empathic soul.

Raven Digitalis Author of Esoteric Empathy

Artistic Expression – Witches, magicians, and empaths are all natural artists. The process of creating art of any type brings energy from the internal to the external. When expressing ourselves, we can find that our psyches and our spirits get a chance to project emotionally energy outward rather than staying locked inside. Art can take any form imaginable; it is between you and the Powers That Be.

Ritualistically Alchemize – Empaths have the ability to not only absorb energy, but to transmute it. Contrary to popular belief, empathy is not merely absorptive, but can also be projective. Do you ever notice that you can literally change the mood of an entire room simply by your very presence? That's an empathic trait and is magick in action. So, take it to the next level by choosing to utilize emotion-based alchemy in a ritualistic setting when you are feeling overloaded or overly negative. Cast a circle or use visualization to construct a sacred space. Place an image, an object, or a deity's statue in front of you that represents transformation to you personally. Sit with your emotions and gaze at the focal point. You may receive insight into the origin of the emotions you are experiencing: are they yours, someone else's, or a combination of these factors? From the right side of your body, project your emotional force to your chosen focal point. Next, pull the transformed energy from the focal point and into the left side of your body. Sit with these new and magically transformed emotional energies, and carry them through your day. Experiment with this method and others in order to find what works best for you ritualistically when working to alleviate emotional stress.

Serve the World – Empathy's greatest gift is that of connecting with others. We are natural healers. When we are in a balanced state, we can help facilitate unity and understanding in those around us. We can choose to express this energy with others not only socially, but also through charitable volunteer work, educational activities, vocational social work, art, political activism, and the healing arts. We can also dedicate ourselves to support strictly progressive and earth-conscious companies with our everyday consumer purchases.

IMAGE CREDIT
The Green Man Sees - Digital Photography
Tarek v. Bergmann
ceirtdruid@gmail.com .
https://www.ephotozine.com/user/lv426-95967

NEPTUNES SCEPTER
Part 2 of our Erotic Pagan Fiction by DD Scarlet

Welcome to Salacia, Island of Sensuality.
Our Heroines have arrived at "Neptune's Haven," a bungalow style beach resort on an unspoiled island paradise. Here you can enjoy pristine beaches, hike through the mysterious jungle, paddle in tropical ponds by day or romantic moonlight swims at night. On Salacia, you will be treated to a sensual spa styled pampering each and every day and so much more...

https://ddscarlet.weebly.com

..."The fish became the merpeople... And the merpeople walked up onto the land."

"You mean like mermaids?" Rainaa inquired. "I used to dream of becoming a mermaid when I was a little kid."

"That's because your DNA still retains such memories..." Koa whispered seductively.

"Or I just liked the water and had a good imagination," Rainaa suggested.

"People are still born of water... As is all life," Koa stated.

Koa began gently and methodically combing his fingers through Rainaa's soft chestnut hair, dividing and slowly braiding it around her head and her muscles began to further liquefy under the subtle pampering. "Here on this island, we honour Neptune every full moon by performing the ritual of Salacia."

"That's only... five? Days away..."

"Yes..."

"What does it involve?" Rainaa asked, curious.

"Well, firstly, the cherished female vessels consume a special potion made from the fruit and the petals of the sacred fertility lily - this establishes their willingness to spawn for Neptune. They then drink of this potion for three days... Every day leading up to the full moon they are pampered and spoiled in honour of their special gift. Then on the day of the full moon everyone dresses in the spawning veils and is decorated with shells and seeds and flowers..." Koa tickled her scalp around her hairline before offering, "I would make you look like a princess of the sea..." Rainaa pictured the costume...

"Then we all eat, drink and celebrate." Koa then put his lips next to her ear and in a tranquil yet sexy voice continued, "Then once night's curtain has fallen and the moon is radiating her full brilliance across the seascape, they go down into the water and Neptune points his Sceptre at them and they spawn." Koa gently ran his fingers down her neck, watching her muscles quiver beneath her skin and he huskily whispered, "Rainaa... Would you like to eat of the sacred fertility lily?"

"Am I willing to spawn for Neptune?" she asked as she turned to briefly look at him, his shimmering aqua eyes sparkling.

He smiled and said, "Yes..."

She swallowed, blinking rapidly and said, "It all sounds very erotic..."

"It is..." he agreed as he gently brushed his finger over her lips.

Rainaa dipped her eyes to the side as she thought for a moment... What a strange yet tantalising ritual. ... Although not more bizarre than many other rituals which have taken place around the world throughout the ages. And really, how exciting to have an opportunity to actually take part in one... An ancient ceremony. A fertility ritual! Wow! But then, how would she spawn? People don't spawn - obviously that must just be symbolic. ...And taking part in the feasts and the costuming – well that sounded like fun! "Sure..."

She felt Koa momentarily nuzzle his head into the back of hers, and then he said, "Wonderful."

It was early evening, and Rainaa and Julia sat on a blanket on the beach, picking at a platter of crustaceans and sipping Kava from a coconut while watching the men as they prepared the sacred flowers, squishing the small fruits and plucking their purplish blue petals, and then allowing them to simmer in some more native Kava - just stirring occasionally. In their happy and slightly intoxicated state, they shared an occasional toast, their giggling unbeknown to them, amusing their hosts.

When the potion was ready Koa and Wakana each filled a bowl and sat affront the girls. "What does it taste like?" Rainaa asked.

"Well," Koa began, "I've heard that it doesn't taste that great... Kind of a blend between sweet and pungent. But! Apparently it's better that the Kava on its own."

"Have you not tried it?" she asked, alarmed.

"No Rainaa. This is a fertility drink for females."

Rainaa looked at him as he gently smiled at her, and she naturally reciprocated. Then she observed as Koa filled a wooden spoon and lifted it to her mouth. "Here you go..." She opened her mouth and her host placed the spoon inside and then she closed her lips down over it and sucked the potion from it. She swilled it for a few seconds and then swallowed it, just before shaking her head madly and pulling a funny face.

"That good, huh?" Julia commented, giggling at her friend.

"Oh my god, it's pungent, it's sweet, it's sour..." Raina commented, "It's intriguing..." And then she looked flirtatiously at Koa who was relaxedly stirring the spoon in the bowl and asked, "May I try some more?"

"You certainly may," he expressed, smiling, amused by her reaction and then he ladled another dose into her mouth.

"Hey, this isn't poisonous is it?" Julia asked, and Rainaa, slightly intoxicated, burst out laughing.

"You might have asked that before we started ingesting it…" Rainaa remarked.

Julia laughed too and then agreed, "Yeah…"

"No, it's not poisonous," Wakana assured her, charmed by their sweet giggling.

"It just has properties that inspire female egg production, so when the full moon rises you will have plenty of ova to spawn for Neptune," Koa explained.

"Spawn like fish..?" Rainaa asked.

"Yes…" Koa confirmed as he spoon-fed her some more of the potion.

"Mmmm, it's kind of addictive," Julia observed of the potion.

"Yeah, it is… Where in trouble now…" Rainaa joked and the men sniggered.

Wakana continued the story, "Over the next few days, your bellies will swell with ova and on the full moon you gift it to Neptune."

"So what you're saying is that on the full moon, as part of the ritual of Salacia, we have to go and sit in the ocean and lay eggs… Like a chicken!" Rainaa said through laughter, making the men grin. And then, feeling bold from the effects of the Kava, again she promiscuously lent forward and opened her mouth wide up.

"Actually," Koa explained, "It really is more like the polygynandrous spawning seen amongst some sea life."

"Poly what?" Rainaa asked after swallowing the potion.

"Polygynandrous," Wakana repeated.

"What does that mean?" Julia inquired.

"It means all the males and females spawn together…" Koa enlightened them.

"Like an *orgy?*" Rainaa blurted out and the men chuckled at their shocked reactions.

"Yes…" Koa confirmed as he lifted another spoon of the fertility potion to Rainaa's mouth.

"So on the full moon, we're all going to get together and fuck lipe fish…" Julia said, her slurring plus the content of what she said making Rainaa belly laugh.

"A fish orgy!" Rainaa confirmed, still giggling.

"That's right…" Koa confirmed, smiling broadly.

"Well, okay…" Rainaa stated, taking the notion in her stride because obviously it was just a gag – people don't spawn! She was certain it was just part of the game to help ensure their stay at the island be truly unique.

Rainaa had a few more mouthfuls and then she kindly lifted Koa's coconut to his mouth while he took a drink of the Kava. "Thank you," he said, "Just a few more spoonful's left to go now and you are all done for today…"

She stared at him as he fed her, relaxed and happy from the potion and when it was finished and he placed the bowl down, she reached up with her fingers and touched his supple lips and then felt herself tingle as he kissed them. Rainaa then sucked her own lips, one by one into her mouth, subconsciously wetting them, before laying down invitingly onto the blanket.

Koa laid down beside her, his sandy coloured hair falling aside her face. He curled one arm around her head and used the other hand to gently stroke her cheek and jaw and then her eyelids slowly closed as he leaned in and tenderly began to kiss her.

Rainaa sighed as he gently probed her mouth with his tongue. His own mouth being sweet and wet and smelling of the kava. He was a beautiful kisser – the most heavenly she ever had…

She lifted her heavy eyelids and witnessed the moonlight dancing in Koa's opalescent aqua eyes, making their natural iridescence even more astounding – she didn't want to not look at them, but when his kiss became more passionate, her lids once again became laden with desire and she couldn't help but let them fall shut.

Koa combed her rich, auburn hair with his fingers, appreciating its silkiness; before allowing them to float down through the curve of her neck, over the contour aside her breast, and then slowly down to the lower region of her abdomen. He touched the area with the pads of his fingers, envisaging the ova developing inside of her as he did so. He breathed steadily, enjoying her intoxicating female essence and then he lifted his head from the kiss and allowed his eyes to travel down to where he watched as his fingers caressed the soft flesh of her belly, loving her and the gift developing inside of her.

Find our more about the mysterious merpeople of the Island of Salacia as DD Scarlet continues her Pagan tale with us next issue!

IMAGE CREDIT
http://www.mermanchristian.com
https://www.instagram.com/merman_chris

LITHA
MIDSUMMER
BELTAINE
OSTARA
IMBOLC
YULE
SAMHAIN
MABON
LUGHNASADH

GEBURAH
CHESED
TIPHARETH
NETZACH
BINAH
CHOKMAH
HOD
YESOD

Magick Magazine No. 8

THE SOUTHERN & NORTHERN WITCH'S ALMANAC

JAN - MAY 2019

Sacred Days - Ancient Festivals - Commemorative Dates
Moon Phases - Astronomical Alignments
All Collated In One Place For Your Easy Reference
by Shé D'Montford

Know when and why to work your magick by following Magick Magazine's almanac
All times are Australian Eastern Standard Time (AEST - UTC +10) - add 1 hour for Daylight Savings Time when applicable.

JANUARY

1 New Year's Day
21:50 ♀ Venus 1°S of Moon ○ 07:50
Kalends festival to Juno and Janus. Romans offered vows (resolutions), and exchanged presents among each other. marriages on that day were considered a good omen. For the month men belonged to women and not the other way round. Sacred to Goddesses & Mothers of all Mediterianian and Middle Eastern traditions. The women of the **Chorti Indians** of Southern Guatemala drink water from five sacred coconuts to fertilize the ground on this day.
Strenae -a gift giving festival to a Sabine tutelary goddess, Strenia, who corresponds to the Roman Salus or the Greek Hygia. Festival of Cleanliness and food preservation to joy and happiness for the coming year .The custom, survives in the France.

2 0:05 Saturn ♄ Conjunction with Sun ☉
Earth at perihelion - The closest point to the Sun
Advent Of Isis, the Egyptian Goddess of love. An offering is made on the seventh day of the month Tybi that commemorates Isis coming to Byblos in Phoenician to reclaim the body of her lost love Osiris.
Birth of Inanna Princess of the Earth and Queen of Heaven. [Mesopotamian] A white candle is lit at the previous sunset throughout the night and is extinguished at dawn on Nativity

3 0:05 Earth at Perihelion: 0.98330 AU
07:37 ♃ Jupiter 3°S of Moon ○ the father and daughter align their goals
The Festival Of Pax the Roman Goddess of peace.

The Festival Of Lares Compitales, the Roman guardian deities of cross roads.
Kore/Persephone drama mysticom was performed on this night then a troupe of torchbearers descended into the underground chamber to retrieve the naked image of the Goddess.

4 0:02 Quadrantid Meteor Shower

6 1:28 NEW MOON ○ in ♑ Capricorn - Wait, not the time for business.
1:41 Partial Solar Eclipse;
0:05 ♀ Venus at Greatest Elong (47°W) Extened your view of love
Feast Of Kore, the celebration of Kore, the early Greek Goddess of fertility and grains, return to earth after six months of exile in the underworld. The Epopteia (The Epiphany of Kore) This archetypal vision perpetuates many other mystery traditions. In later history the Pagan Feast of the Epiphany became the Christian **Epiphany** - the day of the visit of the Magi, the Magick Practising Priests from the east, to the baby Jesus.
The Queen of Twelfth Night Ball A large cake was made at the festivities of Twelfth Night, hidden in it. Whoever received the piece of cake with the coin was the 'king' or 'queen' of the feast.
Freya's Feast of Peace – Plough Day The first Monday after January 6th the day when men returned to the plough, or their daily work. 'The Queen of the Banquet' was a caricature of Freya, the Venus the North. The mummers recite this prayer to Kore & Demeter. "These petitions I offer for you, ye husbandmen, do ye offer them yourselves, and may the two Goddesses grant our prayers Long time did wars engage mankind; the sword was handier than the share; the ox was ousted by the charger; hoes were idle, mattocks were turned into javelins, and a helmet was made out of a heavy rake. Yoke the ox, commit the seed to the ploughed earth. Peace is the nurse of Ceres and Ceres is the fosterchild of Peace.'
The **Lenaia** or **Comedria** a day on which water was turned to wine by Dionysus, was a dramatic festival in which comedy was more important than tragedy. *Lenaia* probably comes from *lenai*, another name for the Maenads, and the female worshippers of Dionysus.

7 Sekhmet's Day, the Egyptian day of deliverance and rebirth, celebrated with beer and fires dedicated to the lion headed Goddess, Devourer of Time, consort of Ptah, This is the day wherein Sekhmet's gave forth the Decrees at the end of the reign of Ra [at the end of the solar year].

8 Festival of Justitia, the Roman Goddess of justice.

9 04:29 Moon at Apogee: 406,116 km 14:29
The Agonium, festival of Janus, the Roman god of gates and doors, beginnings and endings.

12 22:26 FIRST QUARTER MOON ○ in ♈ Aries - Don't let your temper go unchecked.
19:47 Mars 5°N of Moon ○
The Carmentalia, festival of Carmenta, the Roman Goddess of childbirth celebrated on the 11th and the 15th

16 The Festival of Concordia, the Roman Goddess of harmonious relations. Great time for mediation.

17 Good Luck Day, the festival of Felicitas, the Roman Goddess of good luck.

20 Celtic New Year, the first day of the month of Luis (Rowan) in the Celtic Tree Calendar.

St Agnes Night a night for dreaming deeply and truly. If a woman dreams of a man on this night, it is her future husband.

21 ☉Sun enters ♒Aquarius Fixed Sign of △ Air

05:12 Total Lunar Eclipse; ●

05:16 FULL MOON ○ in ♌ Leo - Show ponies turn their energies inward for a month .
19:58 Moon at Perigee: 357,345 km 05:58
Kybele The great basrelief of Asiatic Kybele, the wateress with streaming breasts represents the ancient axis of Aquarius and Leo.

26 Australia Day

27 21:10 LAST QUARTER MOON ☽ in ♏ Scorpio - The sting of it starts to fade.

28 Little Year Chinese (Luna December 23rd) 小年—xiǎo nián

30 23:54 Jupiter 3°S of Moon ○ Father, Mother and child align over the next 3 days

31 17:36 ♀ Venus 0.1°S of Moon ○ Father, Mother and child align over the next 2 days
Candlemas Eve - The Triads of Mothers –The High Priestess selects two women who, with herself, will represent the Triple Goddess: A Crown of Lights made of candles or tapers which, are lit during the ritual is prepared for the Mother and left by the altar.
The Three Maries [Palestinian] identifies the Virgin Mary with the Triple Goddess. The Copts even ventured to combine 'the Three Maries' into a single character.
Hecate On the last night of every month, which was sacred to her, offerings were made to her in the crossways.
Brigantia, later Brighid In Ireland an image of Bride was made on the Eve of Brigantia, fashioned out of corn straw around a broom handle and dressed in white. The head and face was a mask or a carved turnip, carrying Brighid's cross, This effigy was supposed to come alive with the spirit of Bride during the night. Offerings of a cake or pieces of bread and butter on the windowsill outside or other food and drink were also left out overnight for Bride so that she would bestow her blessing

61

on the people and on their livestock. Young people would do rounds of the town with the cross and a straw rope eight or ten feet long. At each house, the occupants passed the straw cross and rope to each other for freedom from illness during the coming year.

FEBRUARY

1 Lammas in the Southern Hemisphere - Northern Hemisphere **Imbolc**, the 3-day Celtic festival marking the period of lactation of the ewes.

Festival Of Brigit, Brigantia/ Brighid the Celtic Goddess of healing, fertility, and patroness of smiths. She ushers Spring to the land after The Cailleach's winter reign. Children make hanging mobiles with the day old crosses and use other food items to represent the sun, the moon, and the stars. It is believed that a wisp of straw or rushes left over from the making of the crosses the night before, under the mattress or pillow wards off disease. Strands from it were tied about an aching head, a sore limb during and fishermen carried it when at sea. **The Wives' Feast Day** honours Brighid in the Highlands of Scotland and north England the festival is strictly matriarchal the door of the feasting place was barred to the men of the community who had to plead humbly to honour Bride.

The Queen Comes to the Mound. A procession to the sacred spring, the Swallowhead of **Sul/Minerva** when the spring starts flowing again in February. She heals with an ashless fire in her sanctuary. This also happens for the Goddess of Silbury Hill.

The Lesser Eleusinian Mysteries Eleusinian Mysteries celebrated the return of Persephone/Kore to her mother Demeter after her descent into underworld where she was the wife of Pluto, its King.

2 Major solar Sabbat ☉ **Lughnassad**

Juno Februa - The Purifier - Roman custom of burning candles to the goddess Februa, mother of Mars, to scare away evil spirits.

The Day of the Virgin Mary was attached to Lupercalia or Candlemas, because many candles were lit on that day as had been done for centauries at the festival of Proserpine, whom her mother Ceres sought with candles

Groundhog Day - America

4 21:04 NEW MOON ○ in ♒ Aquarius - Moon now waxing -

Chinese new year's eve 除夕—chúxì (Luna Dec 30)

5 9:26 ○ Moon at Apogee: 406,556 km Moon furthest from earth

Spring Festival 春节—chūn jié (Luna January 1st)

6 Waitangi Day

To the in-law's 迎婿日—yíng xù rì (Luna January 2nd)

7 Day of the Rat 鼠日—shǔ rì (Luna January 3rd)

8 Day of the Sheep (羊日—yáng rì) Luna January 4th

9 Break Five (破五—pò wǔ) Luna January 5th

10 Day of the Horse (马日—mǎ rì) Luna January 6th

11Day of the Human (人日—rén rì) Luna January 7th

11 Our Lady of Lourdes[French]Bernadette Soubirous had visions of Mary in the Grotto at Lourdes. It had in previous centuries been a shrine to the Goddesscult. The herb, which grew in the cave that Bernadette ate in the course of her guided actions, was a sacred in the bygone cult. The young girl who witnessed the visions drew forth a stream of healing water from the mud. The Lesser Mystery of Lourdes, mimicked The Lesser Eleusinian Mysteries

12 22:26 FIRST QUARTER MOON ○ in ♉ Taurus - Watch as things grow but don't over eat or over spend.

Day of the Millet (谷日节—gǔ rì jié) Luna January 8th

The Festival of Artemis, the Greek Goddess of the hunt (known as Diana to the Romans).

Gerald Gardiner – anniversary of the death of the founder of the Gardinerian tradition, who many consider one of the fathers of the modern Wicca, on this day in 1964

13 Providence Health (天公生—tiān gōng shēng) Luna January 9th

The Parentalis and the **Feralia**, the 7day festival of the **Manes**, the Roman spirits of the dead, who inhabit the underworld.

14 Stone Festival (石头节—shí tou jié) Luna January 10th

15 Son-in-law Day (子婿日—zǐ xù rì) Luna January 11th

16–18 Lantern Festival Preperations Luna January 12th–14th

The Lupercalia, the festival of Lupa, The She-Wolf which suckled Romulus and Remus, and Faunus, the Roman god of flocks, fertility and wild nature Priests (called the Luperci) wearing skins walked through the streets of Rome and hit the spectators with belts made from goat skin

St Valentine is the name of a singing Christian priest that fell in love with a pagan emperors daughter and was condemned to death for wanting to be 'Her Valentine.' His random and reckless love was commemorated with a lottery of willing young ladies, whose names were put in a box and drawn to randomly be the dates for the years up coming festivities. These were also called Valentines. It was considered to be an omen of later being man and wife. This turned into the giving of cards and chocolates in the Victorian era

16 ☿ Mercury greatest elongation E(18) A new idea dawns slowly Return to the beginning. Time to head home.

The Festival Of Fornax, the Roman Goddess of bread making.

The Quirinalia, the festival of Quirinus, an earlier Roman god of war.

18 ☉Sun enters ♓Pisces Mutable ∇ Water Sign

Spenta Armaiti Festival of women and of cultivation celebrated by the Zoroastrians.

19 9:06 Moon ○ at Perigee: 356,762 km Moon closet to earth

Lantern Festival (元宵节—yuán xiāo jié) Luna January 15th Lanterns (天灯—tiān dēng) sounds similar to (添丁—tiān dīng), or "add children." Many will light lanterns in hopes of adding children to the family.

15:53. FULL MOON ○ in ♌ Leo - Reflection can position you well in the public eye.

22 The Festival Of The Goddess Concordia, the patron of good will and favour.

23 The Terminalia, the festival of Terminus, the Roman god of boundaries and border markers.

26 11:28 LAST QUARTER MOON ○ in Sagittarius - Not time to wander - Let bad things drain away

Day of Mut [Egyptian] the powerfully protecting, primordial Vulture Goddess of Upper Egypt. Some times in her lioness form the wife of the God Amun of Karnak. The HighPriestess Queen of Egypt wore the Vulture Goddess Mut as a headdress to signify her spiritual development, the expansion of her brain, the opening of the third eye, and the blending of her head with the Goddess of Life and Death Herself.

27 01 ☿ Mercury Greatest Elong: 18°E - Communications, distant travels

14:17 ♃ Jupiter 2°S of Moon ○ - Dreams of better this possible

MARCH

1 18:40 ♄ Saturn 0.3°S of ○ Moon: 04:40 Occn - Don't hide your deepest feelings -

The Kalends. New Year's Day in the old Roman calendar. **Sacred to Vesta/Isis**, a new fire is lighted in her secret shrine and

Juno Lucina, The Matronalia - A Pagan mothers' day.

Feriae Marti - The festival of the Gods of war. "The Festival of Mars,"

2 21:28 ♀ Venus 1°N of ○ Moon Female mentors can hep deliver solutions.

Holy Wells Day -the day of Ceadda, the Celtic goddess of healing springs and holy wells.

Magha Puja Day Major Buddhist festival

4 11:25 ○ Moon at Apogee: 406,391 km 21:25 Intuition may be week.

First official neo-pagan church established 1968 by Oberon Zell. The Church of all Worlds Anniversary

5 ☿ Mercury Retrograde until-28/03/19 - Do not plan any important communication for this time.

Festival of The Ship of Isis, recognising Isis as the patroness of navigation and inventress of the sail.

The Pond of the Goddess is still celebrated in the Islamic world, in Africa, and is called "The Pond of Fatima, the daughter of the Prophet." In the procession, one man is dressed as Anubis. Behind them dances a man carrying a statue representing the Goddess as the beautiful Mother of us all.

6 16:04 NEW MOON ●in ♓ Pisces - The dreamer dreams on

11 12:09 ♂ Mars 6°N of Moon ○ - Double protection available to you

12 Hypatia Memorial Day - The 1st Pagan Martyr, on this day in 415 AD Hypatia of Alexandria was scraped and sliced to bits with cockle-shells by the monks of the Nitre Desert of Libya,

13 Witch's Annual Lucky Day

Dakini Day. A celebration of magickal women in Tibet. A Dakini is a female who opens to those that knock (seeking knowledge) - the highest form of magickal teacher.

Birth date of Diotima - Diotima was the teacher of Socrates and was described by him as "a woman wise in this ravel and in many other kinds of knowledge." (Plato, Symposium, p201d.)

14 10:27 FIRST QUARTER MOON ◑ in ♊ Gemini - Don't let indecision grow.

Equirria A festival in honour of Mars, the god of war. Horse races were held on this day.

15 The Festival of Anna Perenna, the Roman goddess of the circle of the year. Her festival was celebrated on the full moon of the first month of the Roman year i.e. The Ides of March.

16 Celtic day of Morgan LeFay which became the Christian St. Patrick's Day.

17 The Liberalia, the festival of Liber and Libera, a Roman fertility god and Goddess.

18 Celtic day of Argante

Sheela-Ne-Grig Day. This ancient Irish fertility and overt sexuality Goddess was traditionally honoured on this day until she was adopted by the Christians as the Mother (or sometimes the consort) of Saint Patrick.

19 19:47 ○ Moon in ♍ Virgo at Perigee: 359,381 km 05:47 Withdraw to your space.

Celtic Tree Calendar Month of ALDER - Gaelic: Fern. March 19 - April 15 - *The Tears of the Sun*

The Alder, represent by the Ogham letter for F, it represents free will, is associated with courage and the evolving spirit.

Hindu New Year - Ramayana begins - This Hindu celebration goes for 9 days

Lesser Pantheon Quinquatria – To the 23 - Day one of five days -

Birthday of Athena but also of wisdom, arts and trades

Quinquatrus the older Roman God of War.

Mabon – Minor ☉ Solar Sabbat - Ostra northern Hemisphere

Pelusia An Egyptian Festival fundamental in the cult of Isis, securing the next annual inundation of the Nile.

21 01:43 FULL MOON ○ in ♎ Libra -

20 21:58 ☉ Vernal Equinox 07:58. Nature balances.

Sun enters ☉ Aries Cardinal Fire △

Ostara - Spring Equinox in the northern hemisphere and was the ancient Middle Eastern New Year's Day

Norouz (New Year) - Persian/ Zoroastrian

Seret, the Ewe - In 2791 BC on March 1st the sun entered the constellation Seret [Egyptian]. The 't' indicates the feminine gender, hence the month of Aries, the beginning of the middle eastern New Year, was originally depicted by a ewe not a ram.

Artemis' favorite animal was the hind. It is for this sacred animal the greeks named the month called Artemi and held her festival as goddess of game and hunting on the first .

Tiamat - In Babylon, Uruk and Ur, the Dragoness of Chaos, Tiamat.

22 Inanna/Ishtar/Belat Their festivals are on the second day month of Nisan.

Isis/Bastet The priests wore black cassock in the service of Isis at this festival. They used the cross as a symbol of her husband's and son's suffering's.

Gardens of Adonis celebrates Aphrodite/Venus and Adonis and the dying or dead lover of Astarte.

23 A Festival of Mars and Nerine, the marriage of Mars to the Sabine goddess whom people identified with Athena/Minerva or Aphrodite/Venus.

Tubilustrium Another festival in honour of Mars. On this day weapons and war-trumpets were cleansed.

24 The Rites of Venus Urania/ Astarte and Adonis at Byblos, all the people in mourning enter a deep cavern, where the image of a young man lies on a bed of flowers and odiferous herbs.

Ishtar and Tammuz. The Goddess descended to the underworld to bring back her youthful husband from the dead. Women mourned for the dead god in Babylon.

25 The Hilaria - Festival of Joy. The divine resurrections were celebrated with a wild outburst of glee. The God of joy Hilaritus was invoked. This became Passion Sunday for the Christians.

Eostre - Easter derives the word from Eostre, Northumberland spelling of Eastre stara, the Saxon goddess of spring, another form of Astarté the Sumerian fertility goddess whose festival was celebrated in Europe at the vernal equinox by cheering "Wassail. Hail and be whole, be well!"

26 Mabon's Day – Celtic

The Requietio of Kybele Demeter and Persephone bring back the life of spring in the form of a tree or a maiden, summoned to rise from the sleeping Earth, not a young god.

The Irish Grey Woman of Crotlieve, a pillar stone set up in prehistoric times is elaborately dressed up like a woman for the Easter festivities. **Khordad Sal** Birth of Prophet Zaranhushtra – Zoroastrian

27 02:28 ♄ Jupiter 2°S of ○ Moon - Masculine issues subside..

28 04:10 LAST QUARTER MOON ◐ in ♑ Capricorn - Ambition wanes.

☿ Mercury leaves Retrograde - Yay!

Spells performed to **Ishtar** for the healing of sick man

29 05:11 ♄ Saturn 0.1°N of ○ Moon

The Hieros Gamos, or Holy Marriage was the most significant rite of the Pagan New Year. Thos symbolic wedding between the king, who represented the god Dumuzi, and a priestesses, who represented the Goddess Inanna... she was to be the dominant partner.

Basilissa. The marriage of the Basilissa or wife of the Archon Basileus, with Dionysus, the Basilissa representing the country.

Ishtar's Day. Sacred to the ancient Babylonian Goddess of Love

30 The Fixing Of Destiny to Mammitu was the Goddess of Fate

Festival of Salus, the Goddess of salt, salaries, greetings, safety and wellbeing. Optimum time for personal protection spells

31 Aradian festival of Luna. Originally a Thracian Goddess of the moon and Magick. The Greeks identified her as Artemis, Hecate and Persephone. Eventually she became the Italian Goddess of the Moon and still has an ancient sanctuary in Rome today.

Mawlid an Nabi - Islam - The birthday of Prophet Muhammad, founder of Islam, in about 570 c.e. The prophet's teachings are read and religious meetings are held.

APRIL

---

1 00:14 ○ Moon at Apogee: 405,577 km 10:14 Let your inspiration roam free

April Fools Day

Veneralia Festival of Venus, goddess of love and beauty who makes fools of us all. Burn some valerian for Aphrodite on this day to aid love. **3 Pesach (Passover)** is the main Jewish festival of the year Jewish 8-day celebration of the deliverance of the Jews from slavery.

2 04:18 ♀ Venus 3°N of Moon ○ -The Feminine rises united together

23:01 ☿ Mercury 4°N of Moon ○ -Don't let your subconscious play tricks on you

4 Megalesia Festival of the Great Mother was a festival in honour of the Magna Mater,

5 08:50 NEW MOON ● in ♈ Aries —Hecate calls the old away

Lady Luck Day Festival of Fortuna, the goddess of good fortune

6 Manannan's Day - Celtic

7 The Day of Kindly Ones – Blajini – Kindly spirits are honoured on this day in Romania near natural water sources.

8 Hana-Matsuri, the Shinto festival of the running naked man. A human scapegoat takes all the ill luck for a year.

9 06:40 ♂ Mars 5°N of Moon ○ -You are safe -

Mordron's Day – Celtic

Lumeria - the spirits of dead family members who wander the earth on these three spring nights. The term Lumerians is derived from this festival and is an allegorical word for "Those Long Dead"

Vampires Day - Christian mutation of the above

11 19:00 ☿ Mercury at Greatest Elong: 28°W - The trixter plays on the edges your reality

12 19:06 ◑ FIRST QUARTER MOON in ♋ Cancer - It is growing. Let nature take its course

The Cerealia another festival to Ceres

Festival of Water – Buddhist statues are washed and then the water is thrown on the followers as a purification ritual.

14 Baisakhi (Vaisakhi) Sikh

15 Fordicidia Festival of the earth goddess Tellus / Gaia to ensure plenty during the year. Celebrated under the management of the Vestal Virgins **The Thesmophoria** – Demeter Hiesmophoria, a surname of Ceres as lawgiver, as the foundress of agriculture and of the civic rite of marriage.

Yom HaShoah - Jewish

16 20 ☿ Mercury 4° of ♀ - Venus - Intelligence and femininity is an unbeatable combination

22:02 ○ Moon at Perigee: 364,209 km 08:22 - Journey within and dream-

Celtic Tree Calendar month of WILLOW. Gaelic: Saille. April 16 - May 13. Willow tree has always been associated with death. In Northern Europe, the word witch and wicked is derived from the name of the Willow. It is considered to be a tree of enchantment.

The Feast Day Of St. Bernadette. (Christian) At the age of 14, she claimed that she had experienced a number of visions of the Virgin Mary at Lourdes grotto, a Pagan sacred site of healing for centuries.

19 11:12 FULL MOON ○ in ♎ Libra - Make your dreams real with magick

The Cerealia, festival of Ceres, the grain goddess

20 ♉ Taurus Fixed ▽ Earth Sign

Western Wesak - Visakha Puja - Theravadin Buddhist– It is the anniversary of Buddha's Enlightenment, birth and death all said to have occurred during the 2nd Taurus full moon in the Wesak Valley.

21 Festival of Pales the Goddess of herds and flocks. It was during the celebration that Romulus built his city.

22 Earth Spirit Day- Wiccan - a day to work with earth elementals and to perform healing rituals for Gaia

23 0:00 Lyrid Meteor Shower - New vibrations exerting that will transport you from your sorrows to joy!

11:36 ♃ Jupiter 2°S of Moon ○ - The father answers to the daughter, the masculine to the feminine.

Saint George's Day. A day to lament the loss of Dragons

Vinalia festivals, festival to Venus when the wine of the previous year was broached and a libation from it poured on the sod to Venus, who is goddess of gardens and vineyards

The Parilia, Southern Slovenian peasants crown their cows with wreaths of flowers, libations of milk are offered to the Goddess "Pales" from whom we get the term milk-pales. In the evening the wreaths are fastened to the door of the cattlestall, where they remain throughout the year.

25 14:38 ♄ Saturn 0.5°N of Moon ○ 00:38 Occn - The hidden judgment

Anzac Day

The Robigalia Festival of The Green Man God of growth.

26 22:18 LAST QUARTER MOON ◐ in ♒ Aquarius - Let it drain away let it flow and go
28 28 18:20 ○ Moon at Apogee: 404,577 km 04:20 Dianna spinning away from you takes away what you don't want. Freedom. Relief.
Celtic celebration of the **God Lludd**
29 Festival of Flora, goddess of fruitfulness and flowers
30 Walpurgis Night The date of the Pagan festival marking the beginning of summer when the old Pagan witchworld was supposed to hold high revelry.
Taliesin Night's (Merlin's night) - Celtic celebration of the High priests of Magick

---

MAY

1 Major Solar Sabbat ☉
SAMHAIN in the Southern Hemisphere. Caileach Beara, a Celtic Goddess, turns to stone. She is reborn on October 31,
Samhain. Beltene northern hemisphere
Bona Dea (Roman) The festival of Bona Dea, the Roman fertility Goddess.
Belenus, the Celtic god of fire and the sun.
2 11:39 Venus 4°N of Moon ○ A night for love.
Vesta "Where the sacred fire of the moon is tended by Vestal priestesses, they are usually responsible also for the rain rituals…"
3 06:26 Mercury 3°N of Moon ○ Trust your intuition with business.
4 22:45 NEW MOON ● in ♉ Taurus — Plant the seeds of the new by the dark of the moon and watch it grow.
5 13 Eta-Aquarid Meteor Shower. New ideas and energy available to you.
7 23:36 Mars 3°N of Moon ○ Work with your health.
6 Lag B'Omer - Jewish. The link between Pesach and Shavout.
8 The Festival Of Mens, the Roman Goddess of mind and consciousness.
Furry Dance Day – Cornwall – Dance in honour of the horned god to bring good luck to your town.
12 01:12 FIRST QUARTER MOON in ♌ Leo - Take centre stage.
Cat Parade Day - Belgium. Europeans parade and worship their cats on this day.
13 21:53 ○ in ♍ Moon at Perigee: 369,017 km 07:53
Fatima - Anniversary of the Goddesses' appearance to 3 children in Fatima in Portugal in 1917, the last appearance was on Oct
Bran's Day - Celtic hero's day
14 Celtic Tree Calendar month of HAWTHORN - Co-responding to the Ogham alphabet's equivalent to the letter H,
15 The Mercuralia, the festival of Mercury/Hermes, the God of intelligence, magick, communication, merchants and travellers.
18 21:11 FULL MOON ○ in ♏ Scorpio - Deep built up emotion rises to the surface.
20 16:54 Jupiter 2°S of Moon ○
Plynteria – Festival to Athena the goddess of wisdom
Olwen's Day - Celtic
21 ♊ **Gemini Mutable** △ **Air Sign**
Maeve - the most truly Venusian of the strong Celtic goddesses. It is for her that hawthorn was named May, or Maythorn. She became the goddess of Beltane in whose honour the May queen was crowned... Her most recent name in English lore is Queen Mab of the fairies.
22 22:25 Saturn 0.5°N of ○ Moon 08:25 daylight occn - Things may not be what they appear. you could be judged harshly for things hidden in plain sight.
23 Shavuot - Jewish celebration of receiving their "Book Of The Law"
24 Birthday of Artemis (Diana the moon) and her twin brother Helios (Apollo the Sun)
Queen Victoria born, May 24 1819, was in her lifetime worshipped as their chief divinity by a sect in Orissa.
The Lama Dawo: Sandup confirmed that, Tibetans believed that the moon Goddess, "Dolma" had come back to life again to rule the world in the person of the Great Queen of England.
26 13:27 ○ Moon in ♒ Aquarius at Apogee: 404,134 km 23:27 - Going out to begin the new
16:33 LAST QUARTER MOON ○ in ♒ Aquarius - Make room for the new let go of the old.
30 Burning Times Rememberance Day. On this day in 1431 Joan of Arc was burned at the stake for the crimes of witchcraft. It is a time to work ritual for religious tolerance and for freedom from dogma wnad the crime commited against others by fundamentalists.

Roger & Robyn's Highlander Handfasting Thunderbird Park Mt Tambourine

HELP PAGANISM TO BECOME A RECOGNISED DENOMINATION IN AUSTRALIA

I am a "Religious" Pagan marriage celebrant.
I am *the "last" legal religious Pagan celebrant* in Australia.

PLEASE SIGN OUR PETITION HERE:
https://www.change.org/p/attorney-general-s-department-allow-paganism-to-become-a-recognised-denomination-in-australia

Our government has deemed all celebrants, civil, unless they are from a registered religion, which I am. However, they will not allow any other celebrants to become "religious Pagan" unless Paganism becomes a registered denomination. Sadly, even though there are many registered Pagan churches and groups ready to band together to become a denomination, the Attorney General's Department is not allowing our application for an umbrella Pagan religious denomination to go through. Thirty-six Pagan religious organisations have banded together to do this. Yet, the Australian Attorney-General's Department's reason for the denial is because "They" don't consider Paganism to be an organised religion.

So, an arbitrary decision has been made, a judgment call, by someone with opposing religious views, hidden behind a desk somewhere, to limit your religious freedom. This decision affects every Australian and Pagan, all around the world. You have to tell them that is not acceptable. Say "NO" loudly and clearly. Otherwise, in the near future we may not be able to hold beautiful ceremonies like this, legally, any more - https://youtu.be/GsQALE_Te1I   and we will have **moved back one step closer to the dark ages** and a **return to the witch hunts.**

STAND UP & SAY "**NO**" TO THAT!!!!

It would be wonderful if we all could show support for religious freedom, of a group that has no dogma, is empowering, honours the individual, follows a nature based belief system, that is highly ethical, has no extremist history and that hurts no one. In fact, during the recent 'Royal Commission into Victimisation by Religious Organisations' there were "zero" complaints lodged against any Pagan group or organisation. However, what we really do, is hold beautiful and meaningful ceremonies like the handfasting in this Youtube clip.

Please show your support for what Australia could loose if Pagan Religious celebrants become extinct with my demise. **Please demand that your religious freedoms be upheld by signing this petition.**

Thank You & Every Bright Blessing to you,
Reverend. Dr S. D'Montford (D.D. HPs)

http://www.shedmontford.com/magickal-weddings.html

THE WITCHES' BALL 2018

Pan gets friendly

Community Recognition

Music by Spiral Dance

2018 YULE WITCHES MASQUERADE BALL.

Witches gathered from all over Australia to share the abundance of what life has offered us and give hope for the future, as this marks the moment the Goddess gives birth to the SUN God. Everyone took part in a magical ritual on the night, the Earth has been providing and fueling us for hundreds and thousands of years. With our hands every guest created a biodegradable mogo bag that we whispered our gratitude, dreams, wishes and desires into Native Australians seeds with and a spoonful of soil. The mogo bags we then placed into the great Cauldron where the Triple Goddess will give her 3 fold blessings and birthed everyones intentions within the light that returned to the land.

NEXT EVENT 2019 THE AWAKENING Imbolc Brisbane Witches Masquerade Ball
Come join us at the Annual Brisbane Witches Masquerade Ball August 3rd 2019, Hosted by Mystic Realms

MYSTICAL REALMS WITCHCRAFT
Australia

A place where magical energies come together, entwining the uniqueness of each individual's own spiritual path to proudly celebrate who we are.
You will fit in at Mystic Realms Witchcraft

• Gatherings • Workshops • Esbat
• Sabbats • Unique and needful things for the craft of the wise

Go to www.mysticalrealmswitchcraft.com for upcoming events and other useful stuff.
Remember to like us on Facebook

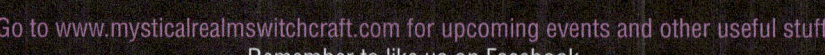

The beautiful, old world, haunted, Tivoli Theatre is the perfect witchy venue

Amy Hanson
Event Organiser

THE SUMMONED
by Olga Andriyenko https://www.artstation.com/asurocks

Protection Crossword Answers

Magickal Dagger - Athamé
Roman protective square - Satorotas
Wishing adversity on another - Curse
Triple Goddess sign - Triquetra
Psychic Vampire - Lamia
Tungus word for a Soul- Retriever - Shaman
One who administers substances for health - 2 words - MedicineMan
The Law of ... - Three
Protective Charm - Amulet
Crossed Swords - 3 words - ArchOfSteel
Protective rings - Circle
Clearing Smoke - Smudge
Banishing Element - Salt
Water Cleansing - Asperge
Powerful Universal Clearer - Sun
Reflected Light - Moon
Protective father god of house and home - Mars
Protective mother Goddess - Kali
Protects surfers from sharks and gives good waves - Hui
A type of magick intended to turn away harm or evil influence- Apotropaic

FREE NON-PROFIT EVENT
June 22 2019
Jacqui Krystal will host a solstice **"Spread the Light"** night of online education on Facebook which is a gathering of minds to share a renewal theme and positive chat. The event link is:
https://m.facebook.com/events/302854207237341

REMEMBER: Go to our facebook page & send us a message about your free/non-profit magickal events so that we can list it here & tell everyone in the community !

MAGICKAL MUSIC

Ath.
With overdriven keys that sound nigh the warring of angels and warm vox that hints at the doom of the gods, Ath's sound draws from Rock and Industrial, distinction being found in subtle Discord.Themes are Dark and Heavy revolving in a Black system with moods and themes driven by Fire and Lightning, all the while drums beating the adrenal rush of Love and Death.
Access Ath free on www.reverbnation.com/ath93

ART AS MAGICK

When you look at a visual image and it connects immediately with your heart, you'll have an "Ahh..." moment. That is Art. It is a spiritual experience. Art has been used in connection with magick since the earliest human civilisations. Art tries to depict the intangible and that which defies description. Art is used to show our connection with this planet and other living things & to things beyond life. Some of the most memorable ancient spiritual art is Egyptian. There are images of seventy-two deities invoked on the walls of the tomb of Seti 1st. This eventually evolved into what we know as the Goetia. The Goetia is a popular 16th century text couched in the language & Christianised belief of the time, describing an ancient form of Middle Eastern magick, which evokes djins or genii. Seti's Pharonic magick was considered a classical magickal text 400 years later when it was used by the Hebrew King Solomon. Similarly, the European Goetia is considered a classical magickal text now. Older copies exist in Latin, French & references to it are found in Greek.

Middle-Eastern Religions of the book ie Judaism, Christianity & Islam, claim that the great god crated 3 orders of beings:

ANGELS - from the Breath of God - **AIR**
GENII - from the Inspiration of God - **FIRE**
MAN - from the dust & spittle of God - **WATER** & **EARTH**

The Djin or Genii are the personality of forces that have always existed on the spiritual plane but have never solidified into the physical. They are the personification of various aspects of existence, creativity & human endeavour, some of which apply to spiritual as well as physical existence. They cannot hurt you as the physical plane & the spiritual realms overlap but are separate.

"No man or Genie on earth created anything, we merely assembled god's atoms, by learning their properties, with their aid" Albert Einstein -19. 3. 40.

The word genius is derived from the same English root as the word genii. This shows that these genii are ultimately a manifestation of your own inspiration, guidance or higher self. She D'Montford is currently paining a series of these beings to illustrate her translation of the Goetia.

The being painted by Shé above is no. 21 Marax, a being that inspires knowledge of astronomy & herbalism.

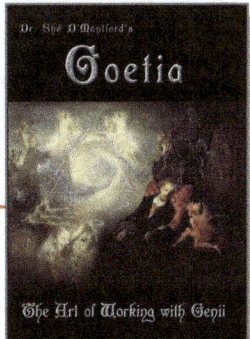

"Goetia" by Shé D'Montford is available through all good book stores. Shé D'Montford is available for private commissions.
https://sheart.com.au/blog

Magick Magazine No. 8

OUR LAST CAPTION COMPETITION
Prize: Glow In The Dark Star - Pentagram - Chakra Necklaces

Janis Ireland 'There's a witch in there and a She as well, people with love and stories to tell. Open wide, come inside. Its Magick Magazine. Blessed Be.' 💜💜

Leah Thompson Lol I bet **Joolz Joolz** is waiting in one, giggling to herself, waiting for the right moment to scare someone

John Walker Dispelling the notion that not every Witch Box contains a redhead!

Darryl Viljoen Done with headmistress duties Minerva McGonagall prepares to transfigure herself into a cat to take a well deserved nap in her favourite box.

Carolyn Jayne "Come Mr Rabbit, I've found the Tea Party" 🐰

Robyn Joy Blackford No, I said "Shé in a box" not Jack-in-the-box!

Magick Magazine They are great value! You never know what is going to be inside. :D

Crystal Clear This is where I thought no one could find me...... dam it lol 😅

Magick Magazine Naughty She! That was not a port-a-loo.

Kane Russell Big things come in small boxes

Simon Court Get out of the box. Now.

E Dario Ochoa 👑 "Pick-A-Boo" 👑

Anna Smith Opening Pandoras box

Anna Smith Witch box?

Kay Maree McCullock Ooh a box, I might get intouch with my inner cat 🐱😂🤣

Michelle Sára Kaldy "I'm finally coming out of the broom closet... or box"

Sandi Lawrence Kenny"s Christmas present has arrived early.. 🎅🎁

Julie Kenny Guess who's mastered shapeshifting? Meeeeeeow!

Magick Magazine Makes you wonder what is in the other 2 boxes!

Mara McDonald "There's a bear in there and a chair as well"

Sj Blackmore This box is a doorway to my world. Come join.

E Dario Ochoa "Mr./Miss Kitty, my BOX!!!" :p lol

Ixchel Cullyn Out of the box onto my broom

Aidan James Bird Beginning to think outside the box

Clint Corrie Get back in the box, or you get the hose.

Rosie Rose And this is "how " you come out of the closet.

Andrew Flitcroft See you next summer says the human-tortoise.

Roger O'Connor Don't just think outside the box, climb out of it altogether. 😄

Sj Blackmore Come join me inside. This is a gateway to the other side of wonder.

Courtney Elizabeth Stark Wow, these subscription spell boxes are really great value. I got a life size psychic in mine!

Leah Thompson "Some people will only love you as long as you fit in their box. Don't be afraid to disappoint!"

Sj Blackmore Pull back the flaps and stick your head inside. There is magic to be found within.

D'Arcy McGregor-Cox "Next, ladies and gentlemen, the great Alfonzo will make the lady disappear from box out of the box #1 and reappear in box 2... or perhaps box 3. Can you guess which one?

Russell Lynagh I'm a martial arts guru but never learnt to box ! Think I'll give it a go. Does this look right ?

Angela Roberts You'll never believe what's in here! Come with me and discover the magick that awaits!

Justis Barrymore Biodegradable Panic Rooms! Buy one, get two free! One size fits most!

Cathy Waples Sshhhhh don't tell the Cat where I am.

Nick Batson "I can even have fun in a cardboard box"

Trev Aahh I'm outa here, don't tell the other two.

Pseudechis T Citizen they never saw her coming

William Bell Welsh Puss lovrs to playvin box es!

Elise Thomas Return to cinder the cat 🐾🐾🐾🙀

Annette Johnstone Come inside, its play time.

Lee Cheshire Not everyone is in the closet 😂

Greg Sutton Coming out of the broom closet

Paul Smith A box of mysterious goodness

Leah Thompson Narnia's fire exit :p

Jen Webster CherShè la femme.

David Tong The portal is open

WINNERS
Justice Barrymore - Glow in the Dark Pentagram
Arian Bird - Chakra Pendant
Leah Thompson - **1st Place** pictured here with her Winged Pentagram necklace, from Spiritual Treasures, a back issue and a little surprise from us at Magick Magazine.

REMEMBER
CHECK OUR PAGES
for more magickal competitions and giveaways from our advertisers, events and other cool stuff
www.magick.org.au
Facebook
https://www.facebook.com/MagickMagazine/
Group
https://www.facebook.com/groups/magickmagazine/

MAGICKAL EVENTS

GOLD COAST WITCHES' BREW
A friendly, informal coffee morning for those interested in Witchcraft, Wicca, Druidry or any other form of Paganism and/or Earth Based Spirituality.
ALL WELCOME!
WHEN: Last Monday of each month from 10.30am to approx 12.30pm
WHERE: Cafe Campanile, Robina Town Centre, Gold Coast, Queensland.
Want more details?
Phone: 0402066330 or
Email: morganna13@hotmail.com

Woman's Spiritual Wiccan Coven of Gold Coast
Live life magically and spiritually attuned with nature. Fortnightly to Monthly Meet Ups. To find out more go to
www.meetup.com/WiccanCoven

CENTRAL NSW EVENTS
Earth Spirit Orange

February
Saturday 2nd Feb Palmistry, Numerology and Tarot readings with Willeen
Sunday 3rd Feb Walk in Harmony to Rediscover Your Inner Potential Path with Willeen and Russell Light Eagle – Lakota Heritage Workshop.

March
Saturday 2nd March Tarot Workshop Level 1 with Vanessa Talbot
Saturday 23rd March tarot Workshop Level 2 with Vanessa Talbot
Thursday 28th March Private Consultations with Max Coppa
Friday 29th March Private Consultations with Max Coppa
Saturday 30th Full Day Workshop with Max Coppa

April
Saturday 6th April Messages from Beyond- Orange with Psychic Medium Jacqui Krystal 7.30pm

May
Friday 17th May Psychic Readings with She' D'Montford
Friday 17th May 6pm Free Talk with She' D'Montford
Saturday 18th May Psychic Readings with She' D'Montford
Saturday 18th May 5pm Psychic Development Part 1 with She' D'Montford
Sunday 19th May Psychic Readings with She' D'Montford
Sunday 19th May 5pm Psychic Development Part2 with She' D'Montford

June
Wednesday 5th June Earth Spirit 11th Birthday Celebrations Sale
Saturday 22nd June 7pm Winter Solstice Gathering Dinner and Live music at Duntryleague Mansion

QUEENSLAND
Ecclectica Esoteric Books & Curiosities

19th Jan - One day learning the mysteries the Tarot
2nd Feb - 6 week beginners Tarot
9th Feb - Advanced Group Tarot
10th Feb - Journey with a Priestess with Siriana

Feb
21st Feb - Night 6 week beginners Tarot

March
9th March - Special Advanced Group Tarot
10th Mach - Palmistry with Kate
Fi 15th March - Gede Parma and Jane Meredith Book launch
16th Mach - Astral Travel with She D'Montford
17th March - Tea Leaf and Crystal Ball reading with Kate
23rd March - One day learning the Mysteries of the Tarot
24th March - Learn to cast runes with Siriana
30th March - Sacred Geometry with She D'Montford

April
7th April - Maiden Mother Crone with Siriana
27th April - Advance Group Tarot

May
25th May - One Day Numerology

June
1st June - Learning the Mysteries of the Tarot
22nd June - Special Advanced Group Tarot

Look who's reading Magick! Nada Muller, TV psychic, on her break!

Astrovisuals
Supplying Astronomical Visual Materials including Calendars, Apps, Star & Moon maps & novelties. Manufactured in Australia.
mail@astrovisuals.com.au
https://www.astrovisuals.com/
0431 193 396

REMEMBER
Go to our facebook page & send us a message about your free/non-profit magickal events so that we can list it here & tell everyone in the community !
https://www.facebook.com/MagickMagazine/

TAKE A SELFIE reading Magick Magazine. Make the photo memorable or in an amazing location. Then send it to us for a chance to win great prizes & you might even see yourself in the pages of Magick too!

Professional Psychic Reading Service is located in Gold Coast, Australia. We helped change the lives of hundreds of satisfied customers from around the world through psychic readings.
www.barbspsychicreadings.com

Barb's Psychic Readings
0450 593 196

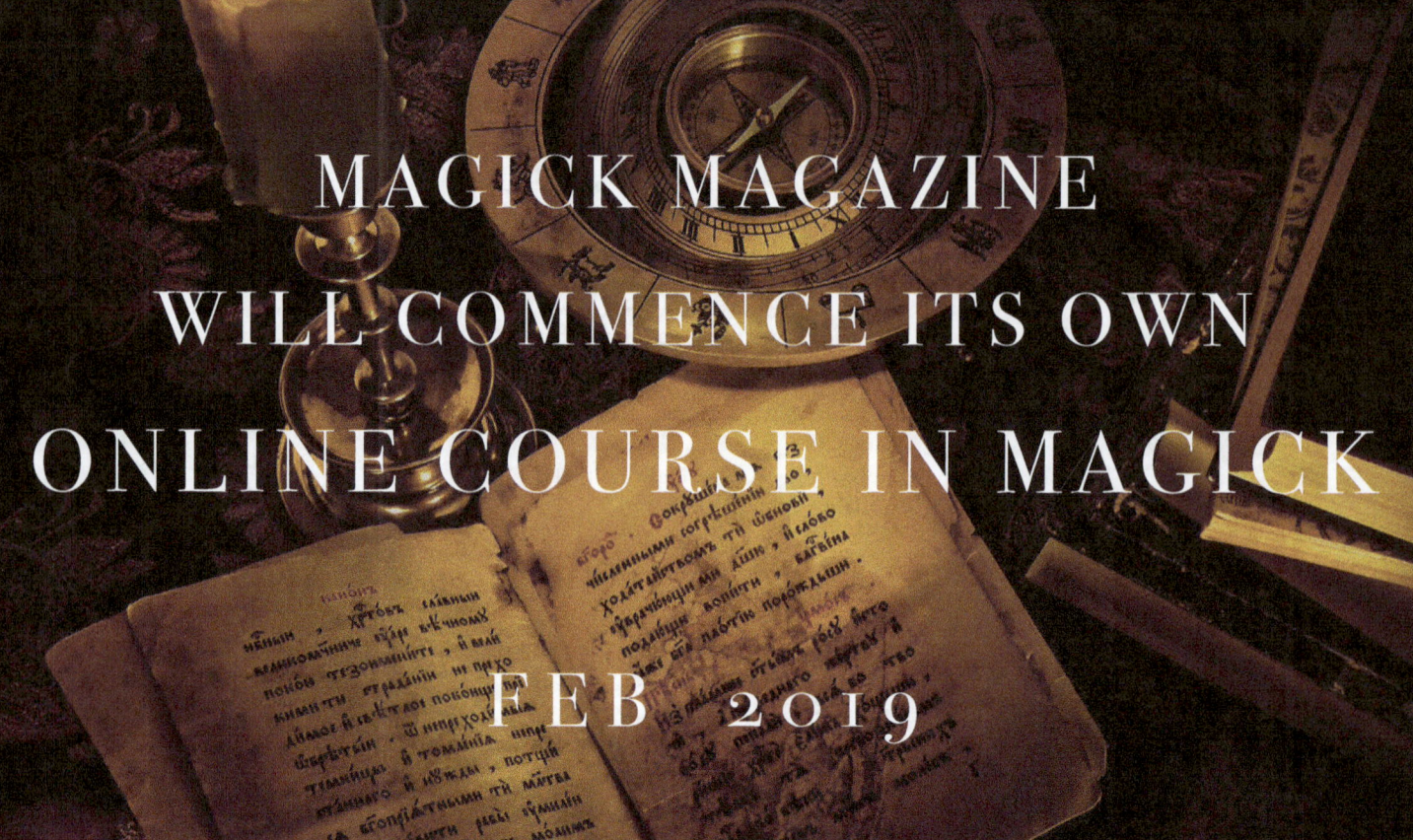

MAGICK MAGAZINE
WILL COMMENCE ITS OWN
ONLINE COURSE IN MAGICK

FEB 2019

EVERYONE CAN PERFORM MAGICK. To a lesser extent we do it every day. Our WILL shapes our world. We make sure that we get the things we like & influence people to see things our way. But we can learn to do so much more. You can learn to do Magick far more effectively. We can get results in a scientifically repeatable way.

SHÉ D'MONTFORD WILL SHOW YOU HOW.

Learn esoteric skills from **AURA SEEING** to **THE ZIGI**. Learn magickal methods from **INDIGENOUS MAGICK** of the Australia Aborigines through to the **HIGH MAGICK** of the elite ceremonial magickians. From **BASIC CANDLE** & **SIGAL MAGICK** through to **TIME TRAVEL & TRANSCENDENCE**.

THESE ARE TESTED METHODS THAT WORK!

Shé has a deep, extensive curriculum that she has taught around the world since 1990. Shé teaches magick without the nonsense. Magick, when you do it right, is not that hard. Learning the right way from a good teacher is the necessary thing. View the curriculum online www.shedmontford.com/curriculum.html Now, Shé D'Montford's classes are moving into the digital age to make all the Magick available to you in a practical & easy to learn package. These classes will be live & pre-recorded, online courses, with the ability to interact directly with Shé D'Montford & ask her questions.

Shé D'Montford has been traveling around the world to make herself available to teach empowering magick to eager students in person. Now, with the aid of digital technology, Shé can be available to all sincere seekers, anywhere in the world, all the time, Packages will bundle together units that are usually about $95 each, for the low price of only $25 per month. YOU can save thousands & YOU can have personal tuition no matter where in the world YOU live, whenever it is convenient for YOU to learn.

Sign up for to our exclusive subscribers group, for as little as $25 per month & enjoy having full access to all that you can possibly learn or you can purchase specific packages. There is a recommended order to the lessons to help you progress. Join up for your no risk beginners course today. There is a 30-day money back guarantee if you are not happy & you can unsubscribe at any time.

GO TO www.magick.org.au & BEGIN A MAGICKAL LIFE TODAY

BONUS:
Every subscriber receives Magick Magazine for free for the duration of their subscription to their magickal tuition.

www.ingramcontent.com/pod-product-compliance
Lightning Source LLC
Chambersburg PA
CBHW080900010526
44118CB00015B/2220